Praise for Dr. Hubbard's work:

"...In *The Diversity Scorecard* Dr. Hubbard takes us from theory to practice. His metrics cover demographics, climate, internal/external diversity, and suppliers. While most works focus on one particular sector this book uniquely provides strategy, tactics, and communication approaches for all types of organizations.... It will be among the most frequently used sources in my library."

—**Dr. V. Robert Hayles**, Effectiveness/Diversity Consultant;
Coauthor: *The Diversity Directive: Why Some Initiatives Fail and What to Do About It*

"...the very best workshop I have attended on diversity. This is world class!"

—**Diversity Director**

"Dr. Hubbard's book provides a unique approach to aligning Diversity Initiatives with your critical business initiatives. Full of practical tools, complex yet easy to grasp methodologies, this book presents a framework aimed at ensuring targeted, measurable outcomes."

— **Je A'nna McCardie**

"Dr. Hubbard has written a practical, straight-forward book which provides a roadmap to help people manage and measure diversity performance. What makes this book especially worthwhile is that he conveys his ideas in terms that line managers and senior executives will understand and that is how diversity adds value to organization performance and the bottom line."

— **Emilio Egea,** Vice President Human Resources
Prudential Financial

"Dr. Hubbard's measurement techniques and methodologies were instrumental in helping tie our diversity initiatives to our organization's business objectives and strategies."

—**Diversity Office Leader**

"Diversity practitioners desiring to ... enhance their thinking about "Diversity measurements," will find Ed Hubbard's latest work to be helpful. Without a doubt, this book is a significant contribution to the continuing evolution of the discussion about measurements and Diversity."

— **Dr. R. Roosevelt Thomas**, President
American Institute for Managing Diversity

Essential Reading on Diversity
by Edward E. Hubbard, Ph.D.

Measuring Diversity Results

How to Calculate Diversity Return on Investment

The Diversity Scorecard:
Evaluating the Impact of Diversity
on Organizational Performance

Implementing Diversity Measurement and Management
Casebook Volume 1 of the Diversity in Practice series
edited by Dr. Edward Hubbard

The Manager's Pocket Guide to Diversity Management

The Diversity Discipline

Diversity Performance Consulting
publishing in 2009

Measuring the ROI Impact of Diversity Training
Publishing in 2009

The Hidden Side of Employee Resistance to Change
revised and updated 2009

THE DIVERSITY DISCIPLINE

Implementing Diversity
Work with a Strategy,
Structure, and ROI
Measurement Focus

by

EDWARD E. HUBBARD, PH.D.

Global Insights Publishing
1302 Holm Road
Petaluma, CA 94954
Office: (707) 763-8380   Fax: (707) 763-3640
Web: hubbardNhubbardinc.com
Products Web: hubbardscupboard.meridian1.net

The DIVERSITY DISCIPLINE

Implementing Diversity
Work with a Strategy,
Structure, and ROI
Measurement Focus

by

EDWARD E. HUBBARD, PH.D.

Contents at a Glance

FIGURES, TABLES, AND ILLUSTRATIONS

Preface

Diversity is a growing area of interest and specialization for many professionals in corporations, nonprofits, social services, faith-based organizations, and government agencies, therefore the discussion of a Diversity Discipline Framework™, roles, competencies, credentials and certification is both important and necessary to maintain and enhance the credibility of the field. Individuals and organizations are asking:

▶ What kind of specialized training is required?

▶ What level of proficiency must diversity practitioners achieve to be fully capable and credible?

▶ What are the roles, areas of expertise and levels of competence needed to qualify as a certified diversity professional?

▶ What role structure is critical for the diversity department's success in this organization?

▶ How do I assess my effectiveness as a strategic business partner?

▶ How do I gauge the progress of our organization's diversity change initiative in business and mission-based measurement terms?

▶ How do I calculate the Diversity Return on Investment (DROI®) impact of our initiatives that reflect credibility?

▶ How do I influence decision making for organizational

improvement using effective diversity strategies and methods?

▶ What skills and competencies do I need to communicate our diversity progress in business-aligned terms?

▶ How do we recognize and benchmark our work against the most effective strategic diversity models?

▶ How do we integrate diversity into the fabric of the way the organization does business?

These questions deserve an answer.

I have always thought of diversity as a professional discipline and field of study. However, if it is to be taken seriously as a discipline and field of study, it must possess a structure, framework and critical components that are consistent with other serious disciplines. For example, if we examine the disciplines of Marketing, Sales Operations, and the like, we would find they all have well-defined competencies, proven theories, and applied sciences that under gird their application. These theories and sciences provide a recognized structure, strategy and a set of measurable standards to guide those who work in the field.

If we examine the disciplines that include doctors, engineers, lawyers, and others, they must be certified to practice their craft. There are also certifications for human resource professionals such as the PHR and SPHR certifications offered by the Society for Human Resource Management (SHRM) for Human Resource Professionals, the HPI certification for Trainers by the American Society for Training and Development (ASTD), or the CPT certification for Organization Development professionals offered by the International Society for Performance Improvement (ISPI).

The Hubbard Diversity Measurement and Productivity (HDM&P) Institute offers six diversity certifications based in its Diversity ROI® and Diversity ROI Analytics® methodology:

▶ Certified Diversity Trainer® (CDT)

▶ Certified Diversity Advisor® (CDA)

▶ Certified Diversity Performance Consultant® (CDPC)

▶ Certified Diversity Business Partner® (CDBP)

▶ Certified Diversity Strategist® (CDS)

▶ Certified Diversity Intervention Specialist® (CDIS)

These fields of study contain specific, identifiable roles that are performed, areas of expertise that allow a practitioner to build specialized concentrations of skills and knowledge within the discipline, detailed outputs produced by these roles, as well as a model of measurable competencies that define specific behaviors that enable the work to be completed with a high degree of accuracy and effectiveness. As a professional discipline, diversity must operate with similar standards built on a solid framework of both concept and science that is delivered through the work of competent, credible diversity professionals using clear standards of excellence linked to business performance. Using their talents and skills, based upon a competency-rich Diversity Discipline Framework™, diversity professionals will be able to integrate the ideas underlying diversity with specific measurement and other strategies and organizational systems theory to help create a diversity-enriched climate that utilizes diverse resources more effectively.

This book highlights a proven framework in use by the Hubbard Diversity Measurement and Productivity (HDM&P) Institute. Its intent is to offer a resource, guidance and potential standards of excellence to individuals and organizations who share a vision of diversity as a credible, professional discipline and field of study. The Hubbard Diversity Discipline Framework™ offers additional insight and tools to use along this journey.

Chapter One describes why diversity should be considered a professional discipline by definition and highlights the Hubbard Diversity Measurement and Productivity (HDM&P) Institute's competency model for training diversity practitioners. It explores some of the basic definitions of diversity used to support the work and explores the professional practice of diversity along with implications for enhancing the profession's credibility with credentials.

Chapter Two describes the Hubbard Diversity Discipline Framework™ and each of its specific components. It outlines four primary Diversity Performance Impact Roles that drive the profession along with identified Diversity Areas of Expertise (DAOE's), as well as behaviorally specific skills and competencies needed to perform each role. This chapter also highlights a five-stage diversity strategic change model to help transition and transform the organization into a high performing organization using diversity. Chapters Three through Five expands upon each component of the framework in detail.

Chapter Six provides a primer on diversity measurement and the Hubbard Diversity ROI (DROI®) model and process whereas Chapter Seven explains a five-level measurement taxonomy to clarify the operating performance levels of a diversity intervention and to further define the meaning of "diversity levels of evaluation."

Chapter Eight outlines strategic applications and uses of the Hubbard Diversity Discipline Framework™. It explains how Chief Diversity Officers (CDO's) and Individual contributors can use the framework for applications such as selection, training, development and more.

Chapter Nine provides guidelines and techniques for maximizing diversity's ROI performance and value. It also explains some of the measurement and evaluation schemes that have been used historically. It details the criteria for an effective ROI process, a list of measurement guiding principles, barriers to implementation and cautions when measuring ROI.

Finally, Chapter Ten outlines key considerations for sustaining the diversity profession by developing diversity maturity in all aspects of the Hubbard Diversity Discipline Framework™, building diversity ROI measurement communities of practice and highlighting a few global trends.

Acknowledgements

My first and deepest appreciation goes to my beautiful, caring wife, Myra. Your love, support, and helpful perspectives along the way made this work possible. You give me the hope and courage to continue to do this work in spite of the difficulties and challenges. This writing period was especially challenging and I could not have made it through this project without God's love and yours. This book is dedicated to you.

Secondly, I would like to thank my wonderful family. My mother, Geneva Hubbard whose love and encouragement always keeps me strong and whose wisdom is so vast its immeasurable. To my sisters and their families as well as a host of relatives who always kept me in their prayers. To Sheila and Phillip Parks, Pearl, Pastor Shane and Tammy Wallis, Gary & Michelle Hughes, Lloyd and Cathy Yarbourough, and our church family at Harvest Christian Assembly as well as many others too numerous to list…
Thank You.

There are a number of people, whether they know it or not, who made the completion of this book possible. Some of them provided their scholarly works. Others provided personal encouragement.

I am again indebted to the many scholars on measurement such as Drs. Jack J. and Patti Pullium Phillips, Ron Drew Stone, Holly Burkett, Dr. Jac Fitz-enz, researchers at ASTD, SHRM, ISPI and others too numerous to mention. Their thought-provoking research helped shape some of the major processes utilized in this framework and approach. Thank you for sharing your knowledge such that others can learn and grow.

I am particularly indebted to several diversity professionals. I would also like to thank my great colleague and friend, Emilio Egea for your terrific insights and always having my back when I needed it most. I want to thank all of the members of the Diversity Collegium, participant in the many Hubbard Diversity Measurement & Productivity Institute programs, particularly the "Measuring Diversity Results," "Diversity Scorecard," "Diversity ROI certification" workshops, and others too numerous to name.

To my friend, Dolores Gillum of Kathexis Design for her brilliant, creative work on this book and everything she touches. You are truly gifted. Thank you for your hard work.

And of course, to our tremendous Hubbard & Hubbard, Inc., staff, particularly Sarah Holmberg, and Belinda Farnsworth whose support and hard work helped keep things running smoothly during this period.

In any work like this, there are many people whose contributions deserve recognition that I may have overlooked. Please forgive me if I missed you in this list. Thank you all for your guidance, love, and support.

Edward E. Hubbard
August, 2008
Petaluma, California

CHAPTER 1

Diversity Work is a Professional Discipline!

Introduction

Having a defined set of competencies is a hallmark of a true professional discipline. Thus, it is a given that the practice of creating and supporting a competency model is a key role in any organized professional industry based upon that discipline. *The American Heritage Dictionary* defines a "**discipline**" as "a state of order based upon submission to rules and authority; a set of rules or methods such as those regulating a practice; training that is expected to produce a specific character or pattern of behavior, especially that which is expected to produce moral or mental improvement." *Webster's New Universal Unabridged Dictionary* defines an "**industry**" as a section of the economy concerned with production. It is also defined as an "earnest, steady effort; constant diligence in application to work; systematic work, habitual employment; intelligent work; skill; an application of this." From my point of view as founder of the Hubbard Diversity Measurement and Productivity (HDM&P) Institute, the discipline of diversity and its practice as an industrial producer of improved organizational performance meets all of these definitional requirements.

Diversity work is both a "discipline" requiring a state of order based upon submission to rules and authority; a set of rules or methods that are regulated as a professional practice. And it is a full fledged "industry" characterized by its operation as an element of our economy concerned with production. The diversity discipline also reflects an earnest, steady effort; constant diligence in application to work in an organization that is systematic, habitual intelligent work requiring an application of specific skills and competencies.

For the past 14 years, we have operated the Hubbard Diversity Measurement and Productivity (HDM&P) Institute with competency models that define standards of excellence for the diversity professionals we trained. As the HDM&P Institute has grown, we incorporated new thinking and skill-based approaches. Each HDM&P competency model we developed marked a milestone in the expansion of the field from a singular focus on diversity awareness training to a focus on human capital asset management and strategic performance improvement. This book seeks to raise the bar in the diversity field. It provides a framework of competencies diversity professionals and organizations need today and will need in the future.

This book is designed primarily to help diversity professionals and others interested in implementing diversity work with a strategy, structure and return on investment (DROI®) focus. It is based upon the conceptual framework and structure I developed for the Hubbard Diversity Measurement and Productivity (HDM&P) Institute. It presents a model and framework used for structuring and certifying diversity professionals who attend HDM&P workshops based upon clearly defined roles, expertise areas, and competencies. We believe that diversity work must be based upon proven theories and applied sciences like any other discipline. This book will guide you through the competency and skill-based credentials framework needed to assess your individual skills and/or your organization's diversity department structure.

It also contains a new competency model and diversity measurement taxonomy that defines the diversity profession in the context of its strategic contribution to performance. It addresses the need for the profession to balance its work to build diverse and inclusive work environments with the organization's need for performance and results. This book will help you...

► Identify four primary roles that have a tremendous impact on the structure and credible practice of the diversity profession

► Describe a competency model and diversity measurement taxonomy that is comprehensive, inspiring, and results-oriented

► Provide a foundation and strategies for utilizing competency-based applied science applications, producing deliverables, and increasing diversity performance outputs

▶ Learn techniques and approaches to implement the diversity disciple to address key organization challenges

▶ Maximize diversity's ROI performance and value

Perhaps when you think of diversity, you think of programs and initiatives employed in organizations, communities, agencies, and schools rather than as an entire discipline of study. You may associate diversity with the principle of respect or simply think of it as race relations. You may broadly define diversity as another name for human differences such as race, ethnicity, gender, age, sexual orientation, religion, occupational role and status, mental and physical ability, and the numbers of ways in which human beings are different. If you did, you would be partially correct with any of these thoughts — the field of diversity and diversity management is broad and is most often experienced in practice rather than studied as a discipline. Yet it is a field of professional practice as well as an area of systematic study and applied scientific inquiry. The field of diversity and diversity management is rooted in several disciplines — the behavioral sciences, business, and education. The domain of the field focuses on multiple levels of human systems — the individual, interpersonal, organizational, and societal (Plummer, 2003).

Diversity Defined for the Purposes of this Book

Diversity can be defined as a collective mixture characterized by differences and similarities that are applied in pursuit of organizational objectives (Thomas, 1996, 1999). Diversity management is the process of planning for, organizing, directing, and supporting these collective mixtures in a way that adds a measurable difference to organizational performance (Hubbard, 2004). These definitions will serve as high level organizing frames for viewing the focus of diversity work throughout this book.

It is also important to note that diversity is multidimensional and complex. It can be organized into four interdependent and sometimes overlapping aspects that contain these aforementioned mixtures: Workforce Diversity, Behavioral Diversity, Structural Diversity, and Business and Global Diversity.

Workforce Diversity encompasses group and situational identities of the organization's employees (*i.e.*, gender, race, ethnicity, religion, sexual orientation, physical ability, age, family status, economic background and status, and geographical background and status). It also includes changes in the labor market demographics. Currently, a large majority of organizations limit their diversity measurement to this area, with race and gender receiving the bulk of the effort.

Behavioral Diversity encompasses collective mixtures including work styles, thinking styles, learning styles, communication styles, aspirations, beliefs/value system, as well as changes in employees' attitudes and expectations. Measuring this aspect of diversity can provide major opportunities for improving individual and work team performance.

Structural Diversity encompasses interaction mixtures across functions, across organizational levels in the hierarchy, across divisions and between parent companies and subsidiaries, and across organizations engaged in strategic alliances and cooperative ventures. It also includes reorganizations, acquisitions and mergers. As organizations attempt to become more flexible, less layered, more team-based, and more multi- and cross-functional, measuring this type of diversity will require more attention.

Business and Global Diversity encompasses collective mixtures that include the expansion and segmentation of customer markets, the diversification of products and services offered, and the variety of operating environments in which organizations work and compete (*i.e.*, legal and regulatory context, labor market realities, community and societal expectations/relationships, business cultures and norms). Increasing competitive pressures, globalization, rapid advances in product technologies, changing demographics in the customer bases both within domestic markets and across borders, and shifts in business/government relationships all signal a need to measure an organization's response and impact on business diversity.

As you can see, diversity is a mosaic of mixtures that includes everyone, representing their differences and similarities, and the variety of processes, systems, and aspects of the global environment in which an organization must respond. An organization's inherent bias about diversity can cloud the definition and is often reflected in the way it is positioned and defined by executives and managers. When executives and managers have not internalized the important message that diversity includes everyone, their comments frequently imply that "white males need not apply." In many organizations, diversity has been positioned to focus on women and people of color therefore a "diverse person" in such an organization cannot be a white man. This is a very limited view of diversity and its potential. In reality, diversity and inclusion focuses on the utilization of all human capital assets and entities that drive organizational performance.

Some organizations use diversity as a shorthand for a variety of characteristics such as learning style, individual thinking style, and so on, but often leave out issues of differences involving race, gender, age, physical abilities, sexual orientation, functional differences, customer markets, productivity, and the like. In any event, the definitions are less comprehensive than they should be to address the real opportunities and complex issues that diversity offers.

Given today's workplace and marketplace challenges, with fierce competition for talent and market share, market pressures for responsiveness, the need for innovation and performance, diversity offers many opportunities and advantages. A competent and skilled diversity professional is needed to help the entire organization clearly understand what diversity and diversity management truly means. He or she must help the organization realize that diversity and inclusion involves everyone. Therefore, we must examine aspects of the organization's structure and functioning that are typically not considered to understand the true power of utilizing diversity and inclusion.

The Diversity Industry

The "diversity industry" is currently a multi-billion dollar area of focus in corporate America, government, military agencies, educational institutions, and faith-based and non-profit organizations. The importance of addressing diversity in the workplace has gained widespread recognition in recent years. Among the forces calling attention to diversity in the workplace are the changing nature of the workforce, globalization, changing customer markets, and organizational restructurings, such as mergers and joint ventures, which bring diverse corporate cultures together. Most organizations, however, are only beginning to evaluate and adjust policies that were originally designed for yesterday's more homogeneous workforce.

In the wake of Hudson Institute's influential reports titled *Workforce 2000* (Johnston & Packer, 1987) and *Opportunity 2000* (Bolick & Nestleroth, 1988) newspapers and business magazines back then focused our attention with stories about ambitious new "managing diversity" programs being implemented by many organizations. Examples of such programs included nontraditional work arrangements, such as flextime and home work stations; education and training programs intended to reduce stereotyping, increase cultural sensitivity, and develop skills for working in multicultural environments; career management programs, designed to promote constructive feedback to employees, mentoring relationships, and access to informal networks; and new employee benefits, such as parental leave and dependent-care assistance. Many of these efforts still continue today. (Jackson, 1992)

Surveys of business leaders confirm the perception that interest in managing diversity successfully is widespread. For example, in one study of 645 firms, 74% of the respondents were concerned about increased diversity, and of these about one-third felt that diversity affected their corporate strategy. Why are companies so concerned? The two primary reasons cited were a belief that supervisors did not know how to motivate their diverse work groups, and uncertainty about how to handle the challenge of communicating with employees whose cultural backgrounds result in differing assumptions, values, and even language skills (Towers Perrin & Hudson Institute, 1990).

Lawrence Bayos (1995) suggested that the 3 D's have generated widespread corporate concern and interest in addressing diversity management issues, whether an organization has 100 or 100,000 employees. The 3 D's are as follows:

Demographics. Females, minorities, and foreign-born personnel are projected to produce 85 percent of the net new growth in the U.S. workforce, while white males are fast becoming a minority in the workforce. In 1960, nine out of ten consumers were white. Currently, it is estimated that only six out of ten are white. The changing demographics of the workplace are also the changing demographics of the marketplace. Organizations are looking at ways to align their organizations to the new realities of their customer bases.

Disappointment. The traditional U.S. method for handling diversity was to bring women and people of color into the workforce under the banner of affirmative action. In doing so, it is often assumed that those individuals possess some deficiencies and may not have been hired if not for affirmative action. It was also assumed that they should be willing to assimilate their differences to better fit the norms of the majority group (usually white males) and thereby enhance their opportunities for recognition and advancement. In other words, to "make it," females and people of color would have to leave their needs and differences at the organization's front door. After a little more than two decades of affirmative action, it seemed clear that the existing model has resulted in females and people of color being trapped in lower levels of the organizational pyramid. Turnover, discontent, and underutilization of talent are by-products of using the previous approaches.

Demands. The demands for new approaches to diversity come from employees who have become less willing than their predecessors to assimilate their points of difference in hopes of gaining the elusive acceptance into the club. With four generations in the workplace, many of the latest entrants (Gen-X, Gen-Y, and Millennials) are less likely to stick around if the organization is not meeting their specific needs. Furthermore, the intense pressure of industry and global competition to re-engineer the organization requires that organizations tap the full potential of all their human assets.

These factors and many others such as the need for world-wide cultural understanding, changes in customer markets and new technologies, global climate changes, *etc.*, highlight the strategic imperative for diversity and inclusion as a field of study with measurable results.

The Professional Practice of Diversity

As you may already have gleaned, the fields of diversity and diversity management are practitioner-based fields that must rely on theory, research and measurement to support the interventions that happen on multiple levels of systems and processes. We are all diversity managers in a sense. We engage in personal and professional growth, and we relate to family and friends interpersonally. We manage diverse interactions presented to us in our work environments and in our society. We work to make our organizations diversity friendly and more effective to achieve performance results.

For years, countless individuals have transferred their skills at managing human differences on many levels into professional careers. Many of these individuals have developed models and frameworks. Some have written articles, books, book chapters, essays, and lectures to capture their thinking and share their learning with others. These factors, along with the changing demographics in America and the shift to a global perspective, have set the stage for the science of diversity management to emerge. By the 1990's, it was clear that the field of diversity management warranted consideration as a field of independent study. Characteristic of an independent field, professional organizations emerge and training in the field becomes more structured and systematic. (Plummer, 2003)

For example, The Diversity Collegium, founded in 1991, was formed in a spirit of collegiality to be an informal think tank working to advance the field of diversity. The efforts of these 25 diversity thought leaders, from the United States and Canada, helped to produce Symposia and research summaries to further the field. A number of colleges and universities over the years also began offering undergraduate and graduate degrees in multicultural studies and diversity.

In 1995, I founded the Hubbard Diversity Measurement and Productivity (HDM&P) Institute with the sole purpose to provide diversity practitioners and professionals basic and advanced skills in diversity ROI analysis, measurement techniques and methods, certification workshops and applied learning conferences for assessing, measuring and evaluating diversity results in organizations. After years of human resource and ROI measurement research (as early as 1979) and years of refinement, in 1996, I created the trademarked Diversity Return on Investment (DROI®) methodology and applied sciences models which help diversity professionals and organizations measure the financial and other impacts of their diversity initiatives to calculate their contribution to the organization's bottom line. Our commitment to and the importance of demonstrating diversity's value as a discipline is also reflected in my books: *The Hidden Side of Employee Resistance to Change* (1994), *Measuring Diversity Results* (1997), *How to Calculate Diversity Return on Investment (DROI®)* (1999), *Metrics for Success: Measurement in Diversity Initiatives for Law Departments and Firms* (2002), *The Diversity Scorecard: Evaluating the Impact of Diversity on Organizational Performance* (2004), *Implementing Diversity Measurement and Management: A Diversity in Practice Casebook Series* (2004), *The Manager's Pocket Guide to Diversity Management* (2004), *Diversity ROI Analytics* (2008), *Diversity Performance Consultanting* (2009), *Measuring* the ROI Impact of Diversity Training (DTROI®) (2009), *Creating a Measurable Diversity Strategic Plan* (2008), and this book: *The Diversity Discipline.*

In 1997, the first Master's Degree in Diversity Management was offered at Cleveland State University, in partnership with NTL Institute for Applied Behavioral Science. And, in 1998, a professional organization devoted solely to diversity professionals — Diversity Leadership Forum (DLF) — was incorporated in Washington, D. C. The mission of the organization is to develop the field of diversity by advocating benefits of an inclusive society.

Credibility and Credentials

Diversity is a growing area of interest and specialization for many professionals in corporations, nonprofits, social services, faith-based organizations, and government agencies, therefore the discussion of credentials and certification is both important and necessary to maintain and enhance the credibility of the field. Individuals and organizations are asking:

- ▶ What kind of specialized training is required?

- ▶ What level of proficiency must practitioners achieve to be fully capable and credible?

- ▶ What are the roles, areas of expertise and levels of competence needed to qualify as a certified diversity professional?

- What role structure is critical for the diversity department's success in this organization?

- How do I assess my effectiveness as a strategic business partner?

- How do I gauge the progress of our organization's diversity change initiative in business and mission-based measurement terms?

- How do I calculate the Diversity Return on Investment (DROI®) impact of our initiatives that reflect credibility?

- How do I influence decision making for organizational improvement using effective diversity strategies and methods?

- What skills and competencies do I need to communicate our diversity progress in business-aligned terms?

- How do we recognize and benchmark our work against the most effective strategic diversity models?

As a field that is defined by the interplay of human differences in interpersonal, organizational, community, organizational systems, and societal settings, it is not surprising that the requirements for what constitutes a professional level of expertise appear a bit fuzzy. However, whether the issue is theoretical boundaries or certification, the field of diversity and diversity management is a vibrant field of study that enhances the presence and positive impact of human diversity (Plummer, 2003).

As a professional discipline, diversity must be built on a solid framework of both concept and science through the work of competent, credible diversity professionals using clear standards of excellence linked to business performance. They must view diversity as an integral part of the organizational system. Using their talents and skills, based upon a competency-rich Diversity Discipline Framework™, diversity professionals will be able to integrate the ideas underlying diversity with specific measurement and other strategies and organizational systems theory to help create a diversity-enriched climate that utilizes diverse resources more effectively.

I have always thought of diversity as a professional discipline and field of study. However, if it is to be taken seriously as a discipline and field of study, it must possess a structure, framework and critical components that are consistent with other serious disciplines. For example, if we examine the disciplines of Marketing, Sales Operations, and the like, we would find they all have well-defined competencies, proven theories, and applied sciences that under gird their application. These theories and sciences provide a recognized structure, strategy and a set of measurable standards to guide those who work in the field.

If we examine the disciplines that include doctors, engineers, lawyers, and others, they must be certified to practice their craft. There are also certifications for human resource processionals such as the PHR and SPHR certifications offered by the Society for Human Resource Management (SHRM) for Human Resource Professionals, the HPI certification for Trainers by the American Society for Training and Development (ASTD), or the CPT certification for Organization Development professionals.

The Hubbard Diversity Measurement and Productivity (HDM&P) Institute offers six diversity certifications based in its Diversity ROI® and Diversity ROI Analytics® methodology:

- ▶ Certified Diversity Trainer® (CDT)

- ▶ Certified Diversity Advisor® (CDA)

- ▶ Certified Diversity Performance Consultant® (CDPC)

- ▶ Certified Diversity Business Partner® (CDBP)

- ▶ Certified Diversity Strategist® (CDS)

- ▶ Certified Diversity Intervention Specialist® (CDIS)

These human resource fields of study also contain specific, identifiable roles that are performed, areas of expertise that allow a practitioner to build specialized concentrations of skills and knowledge within the discipline, detailed outputs produced by these roles, as well as a model of measurable competencies that define specific behaviors that enable the work to be completed with a high degree of accuracy and effectiveness. As a professional discipline, diversity must operate with similar standards built on a solid framework of both concept and science that is delivered through the work of competent, credible diversity professionals using clear standards of excellence linked to business performance.

This book highlights a proven framework in use by the Hubbard Diversity Measurement and Productivity (HDM&P) Institute. Its intent is to offer a resource, guidance and potential standards of excellence to individuals and organizations who share a vision of diversity as a credible, professional discipline and field of study. The Hubbard Diversity Discipline Framework™ offers additional insight and tools to use along this journey.

References

Hubbard, Edward E., *How to Calculate Diversity Return on Investment.*
California: Global Insights Publishing, 1999.

Hubbard, Edward E., *The Diversity Scorecard.*
Massachusetts: Butterworth-Heinemann, Elsevier Publishing, 2004.

Jackson, Susan E., *Diversity in the Workplace.*
New York: The Guilford Press, 1992.

Plummer, Deborah L, *Handbook of Diversity Management.*
Maryland: University Press of America, Inc., 2003

Thomas, R. Roosevelt, Jr., *Building a House for Diversity.*
New York: AMACOM, 1999.

Thomas, R. Roosevelt, Jr., *Redefining Diversity.*
New York: AMACOM, 1996.

Towers Perrin St. Hudson Institute. (1990). *Workforce 2000: Competing in a seller's market.* Valhalla, NY: Towers Perrin.

CHAPTER 2

The Hubbard Diversity Discipline Framework

Introduction

A strategic-organizing model for this dynamic and complex profession must paint a picture of the current reality and also point toward the future; things are moving too fast to do otherwise. It must also encompass the sometimes conflicting perspectives of the pragmatic performance champions and those with their eyes on the long-term benefit of diversity and inclusion as an enabler for the betterment of society in general.

A framework prescribes the areas of professional knowledge and skills that could be used in setting the criteria by which an organization, association or an industry assesses the suitability of individuals for professional membership or achievement of professional qualifications. It goes beyond the boundaries of a functional specialty and describes the areas of skill and knowledge that a 'typical' (generalist) Diversity practitioner might reasonably be expected to have. It does not include the definition of standards of performance as these are left to individual organizations to define due to the many possible variations based on an organization's size, ownership, sector, *etc*. As discussed in this book, the advantages of having such a framework of knowledge and skills include encouraging and supporting the development of professional knowledge and competence and high standards of performance among Diversity practitioners, and therefore improving Diversity's credibility and professionalism.

A framework can also provide guidance to professional associations and other educational bodies for the development of people involved in the fields of diversity management and diverse workforce performance improvement. It can act as a basis against which the development needs of an organization or association members can be assessed, and can provide a basis for syllabuses for education and training programs and publications. The framework can also act as a benchmark for Diversity and other human resource focused professionals to compare their knowledge, skills and abilities with those that their peers consider appropriate. And importantly, it is a means of providing a focus within the increasingly complex fields of Diversity and Diversity Performance Improvement.

The Hubbard Diversity Discipline Framework™ reflects a picture of what is needed for success today and what challenges are expected over the next few years. It's an image that begs the need for a standardized competency model—a model that spells success for diversity professionals and practitioners now and in the years to come. Because the profession spans a range of expert areas of focus, the model (see figures 2-1 and 2-2) is broad enough to cover all diversity-related jobs, but it is not so broad that it can be applied to all jobs outside the profession. It is also specific enough to outline real requirements for some jobs in the diversity profession.

Figure 2-1: Structure of the Diversity Discipline Framework™

Figure 2-2:

DIVERSITY ROLES
- Diversity Business Partner
- Diversity Strategist
- Diversity Performance Technologist/Consultant
- Diversity Specialist

DIVERSITY AREAS OF EXPERTISE
- Designing Diversity Learning
- Improving Diverse Workforce Performance
- Improving Organizational Performance
- Delivering Diversity Training
- Measuring and Evaluating Diversity Impact
- Facilitating Organizational Change
- Managing the Diversity Office/Function
- Coaching and Mentoring
- Strategic Diverse Workforce Capability Management
- Diverse Workforce Planning and Talent Management

STRATEGIC DIVERSITY COMPETENCIES
- Diversity Knowledge and Skills Competencies
- Technical Competencies
- Interpersonal Competencies
- Intellectual Competencies
- Personal Competencies

This competency model and framework also serves as an excellent resource for professional growth and development for practitioners and organization's responsible for delivering diversity-based performance and change interventions. It is comprehensive enough to guide career development at all levels of the profession, and it covers a wide spectrum of roles. It represents a point of departure in thinking of diversity as an event-based intervention with limited strategic value to one that is firmly grounded in solid theory and science to effectively change the level of performance and impact of an organization's functioning.

The model includes three layers of knowledge and skill areas: **roles**, **areas of professional expertise**, and **competencies**. Diversity practitioners play various *roles* depending in part on the jobs they are hired to do, the organization's needs and its structure, as well as the diversity practitioner's needs. *Work Outputs* are the observable results of these role behaviors, while the diversity *competencies* are the skills needed to achieve those results. The Hubbard Diversity Discipline Framework™ includes each of these key factors to shape the skill-based requirements for exceptional practitioner development and performance as taught in the Hubbard Diversity Measurement & Productivity Institute (HDMP).

Diversity Roles

Roles are broad areas of responsibility within the Diversity profession that require a certain combination of competencies and Areas of Expertise (AOE's) to perform effectively (Bernthal, Colteryahn, Davis, *et.al.*, 2004). They are described in sensible, intuitive, and everyday language. Like competencies, roles can be demonstrated in the context of most diversity jobs.

Roles are not the same as job titles; they are much more fluid, depending on the application or the project. For the Diversity professional, playing the roles is analogous to maintaining a collection of hats—when the situation calls for it, the diversity professional slips out of one role and "puts on" another. Roles occupy the top of the model (see figure 2-2), because a vast body of underlying skills and knowledge supports their execution.

Four Diversity Performance Impact Roles

In order to effectively and professionally implement diversity initiatives, four performance impact roles are necessary. These roles include:

- ▶ Diversity Business Partner

- ▶ Diversity Strategist

► Diversity Performance Technologist/Consultant

► Diversity Specialist

People are hired into jobs or positions. Often, a written job description outlines what they are to do. A written job specification describes the kind of education, experience, or other qualifications associated with necessary entry-level skills. Employee performance appraisals measure, over some definite period of time, how well an individual is performing his/her job duties.

But how people approach their jobs is a question of role, the part played by an individual in the context of the environment, the organization, and work group. Roles are therefore behaviors associated with a job. Each of these roles work in combination with each other to form key diversity positions in organizations such as Chief Diversity Officer, Diversity Training Manager, Diversity Director, Diversity Specialist, VP Workforce Diversity, Director, Multicultural Affairs, Manager, Workforce Development, Director of Diversity Management, VP Diversity and EEO, Director, Director of Cultural Diversity, *etc.*

Diversity Areas of Expertise

Diversity Areas of Expertise (DAOE) are defined as the specific technical and professional skills and knowledge required for success in diversity specialty areas. Think of Diversity Areas of Expertise (DAOE) as the knowledge and skills an individual must have above and beyond the foundational diversity competencies. (Bernthal, Colteryahn, Davis, *et.al.*, 2004)

To function effectively in a given diversity area of expertise, a diversity practitioner must display a blend of the appropriate foundational diversity competencies and unique technical/ professional skills and knowledge. The Hubbard Diversity Discipline Framework™ lists the Diversity Areas of Expertise that are critical to the profession. These areas include:

- ▶ Designing Diversity Learning

- ▶ Improving Diverse Workforce Performance

- ▶ Improving Organizational Performance

- ▶ Delivering Diversity Training

- ▶ Measuring and Evaluating Diversity Impact

- ▶ Facilitating Organizational Change

- ▶ Managing the Diversity Department/Function

- ▶ Coaching and Mentoring

- ▶ Strategic Diverse Workforce Capability Management

- ▶ Diverse Workforce Planning and Talent Management

The areas of expertise reflected in the Hubbard Diversity Discipline Framework™ show a wide range of areas that provide significant value to organizations that utilize these diversity specialty areas.

Strategic Diversity Competencies

The most fundamental element of a role, task or skill is a "competency." Competencies are the clusters of skills, knowledge, abilities and behaviors required for success in any job (Bernthal, Colteryahn, Davis, *et.al.*, 2004). Diversity practitioners often use job competency models to guide their employee and organization development efforts. These competencies are extremely useful in the day-to-day resolution of diversity-related issues and concerns.

Organizations, for example, can use these competencies to assess the degree and level of expertise a person has who may be applying for a diversity focused position. They can also be used to guide a diversity practitioner's performance and development. The competencies are documented in a way such that diversity practitioners and professionals can build their own development roadmap. These roadmaps can be used to seek out professional training and development courses and experiences to enhance their skills and abilities.

The Hubbard Diversity Discipline Framework™ consists of 46 competencies organized into six primary clusters: Diversity Knowledge and Skills, Technical, Business, Interpersonal, Intellectual, and Personal. These competencies provide a comprehensive support structure for the "Four Performance Impact Roles" of *Diversity Business Partner, Diversity Strategist, Diversity Performance Technologist/Consultant,* and *Diversity Specialist* as well as the varied Diversity Areas of Expertise. The competency clusters are grouped as follows:

Diversity Knowledge and Skills Competencies

- ▶ Diversity Concepts and Understanding

- ▶ Cultural Sensitivities Impact and Understanding

- ▶ Micro-inequities Sensitivities Impact Analysis

- ▶ Diversity Measurement Skill

- ▶ Diversity ROI (DROI®) Measurement Skill

- ▶ Gender Behavior Impact and Understanding

- ▶ People with Disabilities Sensitivities and Understanding

- ▶ Sexual Orientation, Transsexual, and Transgender Sensitivities and Understanding

- ▶ World/Global View

Technical Competencies

- ▶ Competency Identification

- ▶ Objectives Preparation

- ▶ Performance Observation

- ▶ Written Communication Skills

Business Competencies

- ▶ Analyzing Needs and Proposing Solutions

- Applying Business Understanding

- Cost-benefit Analysis

- Driving Results

- Industry Understanding

- Organizational Behavior Understanding

- Organizational Development Theories and Techniques
  Understanding

- Organizational Understanding

- Thinking Strategically

- Planning and Implementing Assignments

- Business Integration Skill

- Change Management Leadership

- Customer Intimacy Skills

Interpersonal Competencies

- Feedback and Reporting Skill

- Networking and Partnering Skill

- Group Process Skill

- Negotiation Skill

▶ Building Trust and Rapport

▶ Questioning

▶ Relationship Building Across Differences and Complexities

▶ Communicating Effectively Across Cultures

▶ Influencing Stakeholders

Intellectual Competencies

▶ Data Reduction Skill

▶ Information Search Skill

▶ Intellectual Versatility

▶ Model-Building Skill

▶ Observing Skill

▶ Visioning Skill

Personal Competencies

▶ Demonstrating Adaptability

▶ Diversity Orientation

▶ Champion for Diversity

▶ Personal Credibility

▶ Leadership Skill

Utilizing Strategic Competencies for Enhanced Performance

These core competencies define the necessary critical behaviors for diversity practitioners and professionals to be effective and credible. To varying degrees, everyone in the diversity field or profession must display some aspect of each competency to be perceived as capable to perform their associated roles. For example, it is difficult to imagine any diversity practitioner or professional being successful without the ability to *build trust and rapport, demonstrate adaptability,* or *display cultural sensitivities.* Or imagining a *Diversity Performance Technologist/Consultant* performing his/her role without the ability to *analyze needs and propose solutions* or *make accurate performance observations* that are influenced by diversity tension and conflict. How these competencies are used is largely influenced by the specific roles that are embedded in the diversity practitioner's or professional's job.

The following illustrations show how the core competencies in the Hubbard Diversity Discipline Framework™ such as Applying Business Understanding have relevance for both a Chief Diversity Officer and a Designer of Diversity Learning.

▶ Chief Diversity Officer (CDO)– As executives, CDO's are often charged with helping to make strategic decisions regarding business operations such as in reorganizations, acquisitions and mergers and talent development for succession management. They must apply their business understanding to decide what diversity-related concerns must be addressed and the type of diverse workforce culture that must be in place to meet future business goals. Often, the CDO sits on the organization's operating committee to help guide all strategic business decisions.

► Designers of Diversity Learning (instructional designers of diversity learning content) – Designers of Diversity Learning should be aware of factors affecting the business, because those issues may have a bearing on the type of diversity learning content that is appropriate. Instructional designers of diversity learning often need to think of meaningful examples that provide context for the learning experience such as describing the impact on retail sales when customers who happen to be people of color or women can't find products and services that match their specific needs or reflect or are culturally relevant to their affinity group. An understanding of operations helps them link learning content to on-the-job activities such as teaching managers the importance of "inclusion" when building product development teams. Although these designers might have less of a need for applying financial data in general, they would still value that information for certain learning situations involving diversity. Some designers of diversity learning must justify spending and development costs; others need to incorporate financial principles into the learning content when teaching concepts regarding "%/$ share of wallet by demographic group" in a multicultural marketing course.

These are just a few examples illustrating how elements of the Hubbard Diversity Discipline Framework™ are applied.

A Practical Model for Development and Performance

Even though competencies in the Hubbard Diversity Discipline Framework™ are viewed as core to effective performance from our institute's perspective, we also know few professionals will be strong in every one. All diversity practitioners and professionals, regardless of their level of expertise, will have unique strengths and development needs relative to the overall competency profile. Thus, it is almost impossible to construct a model that applies perfectly to everyone. Instead, our model is designed to cover what we feel are the most relevant skills and knowledge areas for a large majority of people in the diversity field or profession.

Applying the Framework for Managing Strategic Change

Diversity is not a program; it is a process of systemic organizational change. Nobody will ever be "finished with diversity." There will always be people with differences and situations in the workplace that require a polyocular view for resolution and performance. Because the diversity and inclusion process and the framework that drives its results involve change (both personal and organizational change), it is critical that a Diversity Discipline Framework include a culture change strategy and process.

Our diversity change management strategy, which supports and is aligned with the framework, involves assisting an organization through the following stages:

▶ **Stage 1: Awareness and Start-up** – This stage lays the foundational awareness needed to transition to a diversity and inclusion oriented culture. It also provides the rationale and business case for making the transition.

▶ **Stage 2: Foundation and Strategy Building** – This stage implements the diversity visioning and strategy formulation process.

▶ **Stage 3: Integrating Culture and Systems** – This stage generates the culture and systems infrastructure building process which is aligned with and in support of the diversity strategy.

▶ **Stage 4: Building Strategic Capability** – This stage supports and guides individuals in building personal and other competencies to develop skills to solve team and organization problems that require strategic solutions.

▶ **Stage 5: Innovation and Breakthrough Performance** – This stage integrates diverse workforce innovation and utilizes its creativity in appropriate areas of the organization to produce measurable results and generate a financial and non-financial ROI.

These five stages help set expectations of the diversity change process and lay the groundwork for its continued evolution and development. It also identifies the transition stages to take diversity to "the next level" for each successive iteration of the field and discipline's development.

Hubbard Diversity Transition and Transformation Stages Model

Stage 1	Stage 2	Stage 3	Stage 4	Stage 5
Awareness and Start-up	Foundation and Strategy Building	Integrating Culture and Systems	Building strategic Capability	Innovation and Break-through Performance

lementing the diversity change process must be change
. That is why competencies for change management
leadership are recommended for each of the four diversity
performance impact roles: *Diversity Business Partner, Diversity
Strategist, Diversity Performance Technologist/Consultant,* and
Diversity Specialist. Change involves exchange: In order to get
something, you must give up something. In many cases, the
diversity change process requires that people in the organization
give up old notions of what diversity is all about and begin to
view it in the business and performance context that makes it a
competitive advantage.

To produce this outcome, the intervention requires a formal
change management methodology (with identifiable stages) that
creates a roadmap for an organization's change and transformation.
We have found the discussion and application of this model to be
helpful, insightful, and instructive.

Final Thoughts

If Diversity is to be taken seriously as a discipline and field
of study, it must possess a structure, framework and critical
components that are consistent with other serious disciplines. The
Hubbard Diversity Discipline Framework™ offers additional insight
and tools to use along this journey.

References

Bernthal, Paul R; Colteryahn, Karen; Davis, Patty; *et.al.*; *Mapping the Future: ASTD 2004 Competency Study*, Virginia, ASTD Press, 2004.

Bauer, I., Heinl, R & McGovern, C., (2003, June). "Consultant Competency Model Role-based Analysis." Pittsburgh, PA. Development Dimensions International

Boyatzis, R., *The Competent Manager: A Model for Effective Performance.* New York: Wiley, 1982.

Brewster, C.; Farndale, E.; & van Ommeren, J.; (2000, June). "HR Competencies and Professional Standards." World Federation of Personnel Management Associations.

Hubbard, Edward E., *How to Calculate Diversity Return on Investment.* California: Global Insights Publishing, 1999.

Hubbard, Edward E., *The Diversity Scorecard*. Massachusetts: Butterworth-Heinemann, Elsevier Publishing, 2004.

Sredl, Henry J.; Rothwell, William J.; *Professional Training Roles and Competencies Volume I*, Massachusetts, HRD Press Inc., 1987.

CHAPTER 3

Diversity Discipline Roles

Introduction

Roles are not the same as job titles; they are much more fluid, depending on the application or the project. For the Diversity professional, playing the roles is analogous to maintaining a collection of hats—when the situation calls for it, the diversity professional slips out of one role and "puts on" another. Roles occupy the top of the model (see figure 3-1), because a vast body of underlying skills and knowledge supports their execution.

Figure 3-1:

DIVERSITY ROLES
- ► Diversity Business Partner
- ► Diversity Strategist
- ► Diversity Performance Technologist/Consultant
- ► Diversity Specialist

People are hired into jobs or positions. Often, a written job description outlines what they are to do. A written job specification describes the kind of education, experience, or other qualifications associated with necessary entry-level skills. Employee performance appraisals measure, over some definite period of time, how well an individual is performing his/her job duties.

But how people approach their jobs is a question of role, the part played by an individual in the context of the environment, the organization, and work group. Roles are therefore behaviors associated with a job. Each of these roles work in combination with each other to form key diversity positions in organizations such as Chief Diversity Officer, Diversity Training Manager, Diversity Director, Diversity Specialist, VP Workforce Diversity, Director, Multicultural Affairs, Manager, Workforce Development, Director of Diversity Management, VP Diversity and EEO, Director of Cultural Diversity, *etc.*

Four Primary Diversity Discipline Roles

Let's take a closer look at each role in more detail:

Diversity Business Partner – Applies business and industry knowledge to partner with clients in identifying workplace and business improvement opportunities to leverage differences, similarities and complexities; evaluates possible solutions and recommends solutions that will have a positive impact on performance; gains client agreement and commitment to proposed solutions and collaboratively develops an overall implementation strategy that includes evaluating the impact on business performance; uses appropriate cultural and inclusive interpersonal styles and communication methods to build effective long-term relationships with the client.

Diversity Strategist – Determines how diverse workforce strategies, processes and policies are integrated and best leveraged to achieve long term success and adds value to meet organizational needs; leads in the planning and implementation of diversity improvement strategies and objectives that support the organization's strategic direction and that are based on an analysis of the effectiveness of existing diversity improvement strategies. The strategist is concerned with the development of long-range plans for the Diversity department's structure, direction, policies, programs, services, and practices in order to accomplish the diversity and inclusion mission tied to the organization's business.

Diversity Performance Technologist/Consultant – Designs, develops and delivers or evaluates diversity performance solutions; maintains and applies an in-depth working knowledge in any one or more of the diversity performance improvement areas of expertise; takes a disciplined approach to assessing individual and organizational effectiveness in the midst of collective mixtures of differences and similarities, diagnosing causes of diversity tensions from differences, similarities and complexities, and recommending a set of interventions; designs solutions to improve diverse workforce performance and/or solutions to improve organizational performance.

Diversity Specialist – This role contains three diversity sub-roles: Diversity Trainer, Diversity Advisor, and Intervention Specialist.

▶ **The Diversity Trainer** – This role designs, develops and delivers or evaluates diversity learning solutions; maintains and applies an in-depth working knowledge in any one or more of the diversity learning or intervention specialty areas of expertise — Designing Diversity Learning, Delivering Diversity Training, Measuring and Evaluating Diversity Learning Impact, *etc.*

▶ **Diversity Advisor** – This role Improves Diverse Workforce Performance, Improves Organizational Performance, Coaches and Mentors, Serves on Diversity Councils or Diversity Advisory Boards, *etc.*

▶ **Intervention Specialist** – This role helps Facilitate Organizational Change, Builds Diverse Workforce Plans, and Improves Talent Management; may specialize in a particular area of diversity content and is responsible for leading interventions and solutions in the diversity content area.

Playing by the Roles

As mentioned earlier, these diversity roles are not unique to one person in an organization. That is, diversity professionals might play multiple roles, depending on the situation. As you could possibly imagine, diversity professionals could play each role at least some of the time during their tenure in a diversity related position. How effective a person is in their diversity related job can depend largely on the importance of the roles for that specific position and its level or function.

For example, people at the Vice President or Chief Diversity Officer level are more likely to spend time in the Diversity Strategist and Diversity Business Partner roles. Diversity Managers, supervisors and team leaders will tend to focus on a combination of the Diversity Performance Technologist/Consultant and Diversity Specialist roles. An individual contributor, who may have joined a diversity council from another function, may actively perform the Diversity Specialist role. A practitioner in the diversity department could operate as a Specialist, such as a Diversity Change Management Specialist, who focuses primarily on the diversity implications of change and transition processes in the organization. Independent consultants are more likely to work as Diversity Business Partners and Diversity Specialists. Oftentimes, their practice will focus on performing the Diversity Performance Technologist/Consultant role to uncover and analyze critical issues for high performance and workforce integration.

Relationship between the Diversity Roles and Organizational Performance Improvement

The Hubbard Diversity Discipline Framework™ includes an Organizational Performance Improvement model, which was adapted from Rothwell and other sources as well as confirmed through expert application, assessment, and DROI® case study.

...ed in the model below highlight the relationship ...diversity impact roles and appropriate stages in the ...ational performance improvement analysis process.

Figure 3-2

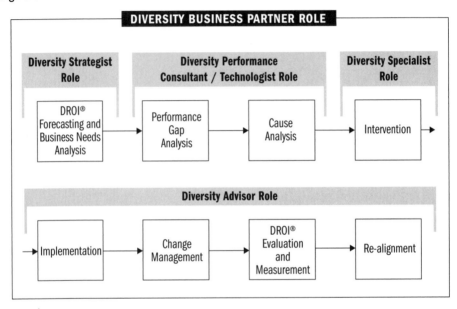

Relationship between Diversity Impact Roles and the
Organizational Performance Improvement Process.

This role and performance model relationship highlights that Diversity practitioners who are certified in processes and techniques to apply the Hubbard Diversity Discipline Framework™ will operate as a strategic **Diversity Business Partner** to effectively manage all aspects of a diversity initiative to create solutions and add value to the organization's performance. They (or in combination with others) will perform the **Diversity Strategist** role to forecast DROI® and/or highlight specific

DROI® is a registered trademark of Hubbard & Hubbard, Inc. All Rights Reserved.

business needs, then operate as a **Diversity Performance Consultant/Technologist** to identify and describe past, present and future organization and human performance gaps. Continuing as a Diversity Performance Consultant/Technologist, they perform Cause Analysis to determine the root cause or causes of the gaps identified in the Business Needs Analysis and Performance Gap Analysis. These processes of analysis help the Diversity professional accurately and thoroughly diagnose the problem prior to recommending an appropriate solution set. Next, the certified Diversity professional will perform the role of **Diversity Intervention Specialist** to select the appropriate intervention to close the gaps and improve both human and organizational performance. During the implementation phase, the certified Diversity professional will take on the role of a **Diversity Advisor** to help the organization successfully implement change and monitor and measure the intervention's DROI® impact. This allows the diversity professional to take stock of and communicate the results as well as determine if further intervention is needed.

Linking Roles to Competencies

As defined previously, roles are broad areas of responsibility that require a certain combination of competencies and Diversity Areas of Expertise to perform effectively (Bernthal, Colteryahn, Davis, *et.al.*, 2004). Therefore, it is important to understand which competencies are most important for particular roles. Most competencies have some relevance for each role. For example, it is easy to see that a competency such as Communicating Effectively

Across Cultures is important to the successful execution of all four roles. However some roles rely more on certain competencies than others. The figure below (3-2) reflects role and competency linkages. Competencies receiving "XX" are seen as critical to the role. Competencies receiving an "X" are seen as important to the role. The strength ratings of these competency linkages reflect general connections to the diversity role. Actual linkage strengths will depend on the specific job description and its implied role requirements to meet the organization's performance requirements for success.

Figure 3-3

The Hubbard Diversity Discipline Framework™ Competency and Role Matrix Competencies	ROLES			
	Diversity Business Partner	Diversity Strategist	Diversity Performance Technologist / Consultant	Specialist
Diversity Knowledge Competencies				
Diversity Concepts and Understanding	XX	XX	XX	XX
Cultural Sensitivities Impact and Understanding	XX	XX	XX	XX
Micro-inequities Sensitivities Impact Analysis	XX	XX	XX	XX
Diversity Measurement Skill	XX	XX	XX	XX
Diversity ROI Measurement Skill	XX	XX	XX	XX
Gender Behavior Impact and Understanding	XX	XX	XX	XX
People with Disabilities Sensitivities and Understanding	XX	XX	XX	XX
Sexual Orientation, Transsexual, and Transgender Sensitivities and Understanding	XX	XX	XX	XX
World / Global View	XX	XX	XX	XX
Technical Competencies				
Competency Identification		X	XX	X
Objectives Preparation	X	XX	XX	X
Performance Observation			XX	X
Written Communication Skills	XX	XX	XX	XX

Legend: XX = Critical Linkage to Role   X = Important Linkage to Role

The Hubbard Diversity Discipline Framework™ Competency and Role Matrix Competencies	ROLES			
	Diversity Business Partner	Diversity Strategist	Diversity Performance Technologist / Consultant	Diversity Specialist
Business Competencies				
Analyzing Needs and Proposing Solutions	XX	X	XX	X
Applying Business Understanding	XX	X	XX	X
Cost-benefit Analysis	XX	XX	XX	X
Driving Results	XX	XX	XX	
Industry Understanding	XX	XX	X	X
Organizational Behavior Understanding	X	XX	XX	
Organizational Development Theories and Techniques Understanding	X	XX	XX	X
Organizational Understanding	XX	XX	XX	X
Thinking Strategically	XX	XX	XX	X
Planning and Implementing Assignments	X	XX	XX	XX
Business Integration Skill	XX	XX	X	X
Change Management Leadership	XX	XX	XX	X
Customer Intimacy Skills	XX	X	X	XX

Legend: XX = Critical Linkage to Role X = Important Linkage to Role

Figure 3-3 continued

The Hubbard Diversity Discipline Framework™ Competency and Role Matrix Competencies	R O L			
	Diversity Business Partner	Diversity Strategist	Diversity Performance Technologist / Consultant	Sp-
Interpersonal Competencies				
Feedback and Reporting Skill	X	X	XX	XX
Networking and Partnering Skill	XX	X	X	X
Group Process Skill	X		XX	XX
Negotiation Skill	XX		X	X
Building Trust and Rapport	XX	X	XX	XX
Questioning	X	X	XX	XX
Relationship Building Across Differences and Complexities	XX	X	XX	XX
Communicating Effectively Across Cultures	XX	X	X	X
Influencing Stakeholders	XX	X	X	X
Intellectual Competencies				
Data Reduction Skill	XX	XX	XX	X
Information Search Skill		XX	XX	X
Intellectual Versatility	X	X	X	X
Model-Building Skill	XX	XX	XX	
Observing Skill	X	X	XX	X
Visioning Skill	XX	XX	X	X

Legend: XX = Critical Linkage to Role X = Important Linkage to Role

The Hubbard Diversity Discipline Framework™ Competency and Role Matrix Competencies	ROLES			
	Diversity Business Partner	Diversity Strategist	Diversity Performance Technologist / Consultant	Diversity Specialist
Personal Competencies				
Demonstrating Adaptability	X	X	XX	XX
Diversity Orientation	XX	XX	XX	XX
Champion for Diversity	XX	XX	XX	XX
Personal Credibility	XX	XX	XX	XX
Leadership Skill	XX	X	X	XX

Legend: XX = Critical Linkage to Role X = Important Linkage to Role

It is important to note that those "competencies-role" linkages that are "blank" should not suggest that this competency does not matter. It may be that this competency has value for that role, however relative to other competencies in that category; it is neither critical nor important in a way that would make or break a person's performance in that role.

The Nature of Roles in Organizations

Understanding the nature of roles in organizations requires acknowledging their complexity. How someone approaches their job, as we said earlier, is a question of role, the part played by an individual in the context of the environment, organization, and work group (Sredl, and Rothwell, 1987). These roles are therefore behaviors that are associated with a particular job. A diversity practitioner's values will guide what roles are accepted and, in part, how they are carried out.

Figure 3-4 highlights a model that represents the nature of a role. In this model:

- ▶ The environment is everything outside the organization.

- ▶ The organization is a system of roles. Each person in it plays multiple parts.

- ▶ Role senders are those people who deal with someone filling a role. They have expectations about the role and behavior appropriate for it.

- ▶ The role receiver is the person who is cast in a role.

- ▶ Individual variables are based on physiological, psychological, environmental, and motivational factors.

- ▶ Work group/interpersonal relations concern small group contexts in which a role is enacted.

Figure 3-4

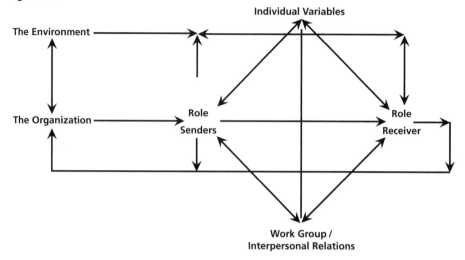

Source: Adapted from: *The Social Psychology of Organizations* by D. Katz and R. Kahn. Copyright © 1978, John Wiley and Sons, In Sredl, and Rothwell, 1987

Though the model may appear complicated, it is really quite simple. Anybody working in an organization is both role sender and receiver. Individual behavior in a role is influenced by:

▶ **The environment**, which creates demands on the organization and may create demands on roles within it. For example, if a new law is passed regulating an industry, it may result in special pressures on legal staff (who interpret it) and on those directly affected by it such as the full organization. Court decisions on affirmative action may create special pressures on human resource managers and those who make hiring decisions.

▶ **The organization**, which has its own culture, norms, and values. In one organization, people might have one idea about the role of a Diversity Business Partner, for example. People in other organizations might have different ideas about this role.

▶ **Role senders,** who send messages to role receivers. They expect certain kinds of behavior from someone occupying a position and do not expect other kinds of behavior. Expectations may stem from past dealings with people occupying similar positions. A production manager may have a set of expectations about the role of a Diversity Specialist, for example. When a Diversity Specialist acts consistently with those expectations, the production manager is satisfied. If behavior differs from expectation, such as the Specialist's concern about improving production using diverse work team approaches, the manager may comment on appropriate role behavior and thus send a message about it.

▶ **Role receivers**, who occupy roles. They receive messages from others about how they should behave. Their actions—that is, role behaviors—are messages that show how they perceive their role and interpret role messages from others. For example, some diversity practitioners take their role as a strategist very seriously. They will be fully informed regarding the organization's strategic plans, are up to date on diversity best practices for intervening and crafting plans to enhance the organization's strategic performance, regularly assess policies and procedures for their "diversity sensitivity and strategic value" for both the short and long term, *etc.*

▶ **Individual variables** that influence both role senders and receivers. For example, differences in innate talents cause diversity practitioners to differ in how they enact a role. A practitioner's personal preference for and skills in creating experiential learning may influence the makeup of activities in a diversity learning intervention.

▶ **Work group and interpersonal relations** that also affect both role senders and receivers. An individual's status and interpersonal skills may influence how well a role can be enacted. Similarly, relationships between groups may influence role perceptions. Some diversity practitioners will have greater success due to their mastery of skill needed to effectively build rapport across individual and group differences and cultures.

This model is useful in clarifying how and why diversity practitioners may act in an organizational setting.

Because of the many roles in organizations, it is not unusual to find role conflict—that is, inconsistency between expected and actual behavior. There are several kinds of role conflict:

▶ *Intrapersonal role conflict.* When an individual's role calls for behavior inconsistent with personal values, it produces intrapersonal role conflict. For example, if a diversity trainer is asked to train a person to do work that is illegal; he or she may experience conflict of this kind.

▶ *Intrarole conflict.* When several role senders have different expectations and convey contradictory role messages, the result is intrarole conflict. The diversity practitioner enacting the role cannot satisfy all the demands. If top managers have one set of expectations for a diversity training program, middle managers have a different set, foremen a third, and trainers a fourth, the Diversity Training professional experiences intrarole conflict.

▶ *Interrole conflict.* Individuals play more than one role in most organizations. For example, diversity managers play the role of management agent but may also serve as spokespersons, advocates, and diversity champions for the organization with higher management. When there is a conflict between the wishes of higher management and those as a diversity champion, the manager may experience interrole conflict as a result of the contradictory demands.'

To resolve such conflicts, some go as far as to replace or try to change the person in the role. A more typical resolution is to gain consensus on expectations. Often, as a Diversity Strategic Business Partner it requires developing an effective, Diversity Return on Investment (DROI®) business case that specifies which roles are critical to produce the performance outcome. Resolution of these role conflicts are essential to demonstrate the quantitative and qualitative value of diversity related interventions.

Building Professionalism

Effectively managing role requirements and mastering the competencies related to these roles in the diversity profession

rated training and work to be effective and earn
matter what your current level of skill in performing
this diversity discipline framework can provide a
for extending your effectiveness in the job or position
occupy. Once you know what roles are critical or important
your job and how well prepared you are for it (evaluating
your current knowledge and skills with the diversity discipline
framework), you can establish a self-development plan to build
your competence.

There are several ways to put your self-development plan in
action. You can:

► Gain relevant experience

► Enroll in formal or informal education and training
programs such as those offered by the Hubbard Diversity
Measurement & Productivity (HDM&P) Institute or its
online Webinars.

► Do independent reading on the subject

► Locate people proficient in the skills you want to master.
Observe them performing this skill and ask them to review
it with you in detail.

► Apply for internships in those departments where these
skills are practiced with proficiency and credibility.

If diversity is to be respected as a value-added profession, every
practitioner must exhibit the highest degree of proficiency and
excellence in executing the primary diversity discipline roles.

References

Bernthal, Paul R; Colteryahn, Karen; Davis, Patty, *et.al.*; *Mapping the Future: ASTD 2004 Competency Study*; Virginia, ASTD Press, 2004.

Boyatzis, R., *The Competent Manager: A Model for Effective Performance.* New York: Wiley, 1982.

Hubbard, Edward E., *How to Calculate Diversity Return on Investment.* California: Global Insights Publishing, 1999.

Hubbard, Edward E., *The Diversity Scorecard*. Massachusetts: Butterworth-Heinemann, Elsevier Publishing, 2004.

Lewin, K., *Field Theory in Social Science.* New York: Harper, 1951.

McClelland, D., *A Guide to Job Competency Assessment*. Boston: McBer, 1976.

Rummler, G., "The Performance Audit." *In Training and Development Handbook*, 2nd Edition, R. Craig, ed. New York: McGraw-Hill, 1976.

Rothwell, William J.; Hohne, Carolyn K.; King, Stephen B.; *Human Performance Improvement, Building Practitioner Performance* Massachusetts, Butterworth-Heinemann, 2007.

Rothwell, W., "Strategic Needs Assessment." *Performance and Instruction Journal 23* (1984) 5: pp. 19-20.

Sredl, Henry J.; Rothwell, William J.; *Professional Training Roles and Competencies Volume I*, Massachusetts, HRD Press Inc., 1987.

Zemke, R., "Job Competencies: Can They Help You Design Better Training?" *Training 19* (1982) 5: pp. 28-31

CHAPTER 4

Diversity Areas of Expertise

Introduction

The middle section of the Hubbard Diversity Discipline Framework™ competency model (see figure 4-1) includes diversity areas of expertise, which are defined as the specific technical and professional skills and knowledge required for success in Diversity specialty areas. Think of Diversity AOE's (DAOE's) as the knowledge and skills an individual must have above and beyond the foundational diversity competencies. To function effectively in a given Diversity AOE, a practitioner must display a blend of the appropriate foundational diversity competencies and unique technical/professional skills and knowledge. The model lists the Diversity AOE's that are commonly found in the diversity profession and industry.

Figure 4-1

DIVERSITY AREAS OF EXPERTISE

▶ Designing Diversity Learning

▶ Improving Diverse Workforce Performance

▶ Improving Organizational Performance

▶ Delivering Diversity Training

▶ Measuring and Evaluating Diversity Impact

▶ Facilitating Organizational Change

▶ Managing the Diversity Office/Function

▶ Coaching and Mentoring

▶ Strategic Diverse Workforce Capability Management

▶ Diverse Workforce Planning and Talent Management

An Evolving Discipline

In the model, the Diversity AOE's reflect changes in the diversity profession over time. As organizations and the profession evolve, new technologies emerge, and individual needs change. Diversity professionals often are asked to take on new responsibilities and readjust their focus. Some specialty areas remain fairly stable over time, while others change significantly. For example, over the past decade the skills required to measure performance improvement and diversity's return on investment have become more important. The Diversity AOE's presented in this book reflect how Diversity professionals currently focus their work and also describe practices that are becoming increasingly important.

The Hubbard Diversity Discipline Framework™ lists the Diversity Areas of Expertise that are critical to the profession. These areas include:

► **Designing Diversity Learning** – Designing, creating, and developing diversity learning interventions to meet needs; analyzing and selecting the most appropriate strategy, methodologies, and technologies to maximize the diversity learning experience and impact.

► **Improving Diverse Workforce Performance** – Applying a systematic process of discovering and analyzing diverse workforce performance needs and gaps; planning for future improvements in diverse workforce performance; designing and developing cost-effective and ethically justifiable solutions to close performance gaps; partnering with others when identifying opportunities and solutions; implementing solutions; monitoring the change; evaluating the results.

► **Improving Organizational Performance** – Applying a systematic process of discovering and analyzing organizational performance needs and gaps; planning for future improvements in organizational performance; designing and developing cost-effective and ethically justifiable solutions to close performance gaps; partnering with others when identifying opportunities and solutions; implementing solutions; monitoring the change; evaluating the results.

▶ **Delivering Diversity Training** – Delivering diversity learning solutions (for example, courses, guided experience) in a manner that both engages the learner and produces desired outcomes; managing and responding to learner needs; ensuring that the diversity learning solution is made available or delivered in a timely and effective manner.

▶ **Measuring and Evaluating Diversity Impact** – Gathering data to answer specific questions regarding the value or ROI impact of diversity solutions; focusing on the impact of individual diversity interventions and programs to create overall measures of system effectiveness; leveraging findings to increase diversity intervention effectiveness and provide recommendations for change.

▶ **Facilitating Organizational Change** – Leading, managing, and facilitating change within organizations; serving as a change agent to help effectively implement structural and behavior change processes that leverage diversity in organizations.

▶ **Managing the Diversity Department/Function** – Providing leadership in developing diverse human capital to execute the organization's strategy; planning, organizing, monitoring, and adjusting activities associated with the administration of diversity and performance improvement.

▶ **Coaching and Mentoring** – Using an interactive process to help individuals and organizations develop more rapidly and produce more satisfying results; improving others' ability to set goals, take action, make better decisions, and make full use of their natural strengths; serving as a catalyst for learning and providing an entrée into formal and informal networks.

▶ **Strategic Diverse Workforce Capability Management** – Analyzing skill levels and competency patterns of core organizational expertise (and tenure) that represent the driving force of the organization to meet the strategic business needs of its customers and key stakeholders; implementing a systematic process to maintain and enhance diverse workforce members abilities to meet current and future needs.

▶ **Diverse Workforce Planning and Talent Management** – Ensuring that all employees have the right skills to meet the strategic challenges of the organization; assuring the alignment of individual career planning and organization talent management processes to achieve an optimal match between individual and organizational needs regardless of background and individual differences; promoting individual growth and organizational renewal.

Some Diversity AOE's may not be seen as important by all diversity practitioners as a group because they are not used as frequently. In fact, diversity professionals are much more likely to provide higher importance ratings for those Diversity AOE's in which they spend more time. However, it is important to note that *time spent* and *importance* is not synonymous. It *is* possible to spend very little time in areas that are essential to effective job performance and business results or vice versa. The primary point to remember *is* that although perceived importance and time spent are both relative to a diversity practitioner's job, *all* the Diversity AOE's in this model are important and relevant for the profession.

A majority of Diversity professionals' work responsibilities can be classified into one or more of the Diversity AOE's. It is not surprising that, on average, most diversity professionals spend the largest share of their time in the Designing Diversity Learning and Delivering Training AOE's. After all, the profession was born with a training focus, and it remains a mainstay.

When surveyed, a majority of diversity professionals indicate they either headed a Diversity function or spent their time Designing Diversity Learning or Delivering Training as their primary AOE. While the popularity of these Diversity AOE's is readily evident, it's also clear that many Diversity professionals spend their time in more than one Diversity AOE. This suggests that Diversity practitioners are often providing expertise in multiple areas and must apply a broad range of skills, especially those that relate to improving performance. This represents a critical change in the role of the diversity professional. Success in the profession is no longer defined by solid delivery or instructional design skills; diversity is truly becoming a more complex and multidisciplinary profession.

Each Diversity AOE represents a distinct area of practice with unique outputs and knowledge areas, and each assumes the use of certain methods and operating processes. Unlike with competencies, an individual does not have to be expert in every Diversity AOE to be considered successful. In some cases, diversity practitioners will specialize in a particular Diversity AOE as their primary area of focus. In this manner, they take on and master this area to perform the role of a Diversity Specialist. Nonetheless, most Diversity professionals will demonstrate a high level of expertise in more than one AOE and would benefit from a strong working knowledge of all the Diversity AOE's.

Influences of Technology

The emergence of new technology has exerted a powerful influence on the evolution of the Diversity profession. Some professionals might even consider technology to be a Diversity AOE. However, it is an enabler that opens additional avenues for delivering diversity performance solutions. Technology without context has little value; only through the expression of technology in diversity applications is its real power realized.

For example, the initial implementation schedule of a Diversity Return on Investment (DROI®) study provides a variety of key events or milestones. Routine progress reports need to be developed to present the status and progress of these diversity initiative events and their key milestones. Reports are usually developed at six-month intervals; however, they can be more frequent depending on the informational needs of the stakeholder audience. Two target audiences, the diversity organization staff and senior managers, are critical for progress reporting. The entire human resources and operations communities within the organization should be kept informed of the initiative's progress as well. In addition, senior managers need to know the extent to which the DROI® study is being implemented and how it is working in the organization. To maintain this level of information and reporting capability, automated systems may be necessary.

Developing diversity measurement strategies, business objectives, and tactics, calculating formulas for diversity metrics, and keeping everyone informed on the diversity initiative's progress can be tedious work. Someone must take the responsibility to develop procedures and a method to systematically monitor and track each diversity measure and set of metrics used to implement the initiative, then summarize the results over time. This task is best done by a computer or an automated measurement system (Hubbard, 1999).

There is a saying that indicates: "If you do not measure it, you cannot control it, and, if you cannot control it, you cannot manage it." MetricLINK®, a comprehensive diversity strategy alignment and performance-tracking tool developed and distributed by Hubbard & Hubbard, Inc., has been found to be an easy-to-use, highly effective measurement planning, analysis, and reporting system that provides all the information needed to help a diversity practitioner manage their role and Diversity AOE by facts (see Figure 4-2). MetricLINK® allows practitioners to manage their entire diversity strategic plan and its metrics in one system. It integrates and organizes diversity measures, strategies, tactics, action plans, diversity initiative history files, and strategic diversity reporting templates all in one place. Mastering and utilizing this type of technology allows diversity professionals to truly perform as capable strategic business partners.

Figure 4-2

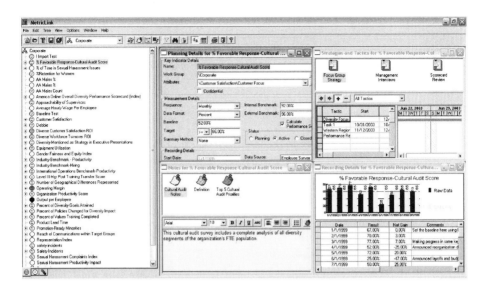

Source: MetricLINK® diversity strategy alignment and
performance-tracking tool.

Figure 4-3

Diversity Human Capital Value Added Report

Human Capital Dashboard

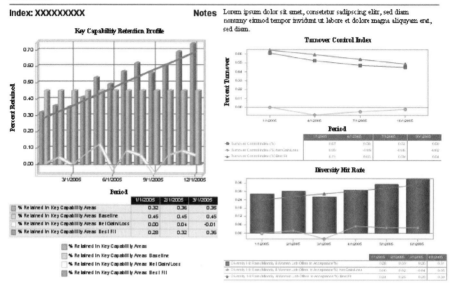

Source: Sample MetricLINK® Report

Figure 4-4

MetricLink Cross-Training Impact Report

Building Performance Capability

Notes

Lorem ipsum dolor sit amet, consetetur sadipscing elitr, sed diam nonumy eirmod tempor invidunt ut labore et dolore magna aliquyam erat, sed diam voluptua. At vero eos et accusam et justo duo dolores et earebum. Stet clita kasd gubergren, no sea takimata sanctus est Lorem ipsum dolor sit amet. Lorem ipsum dolor sit amet, consetetur sadipscing elitr, sed diam

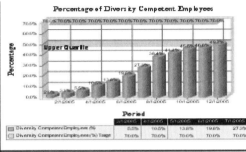

Percentage of Diversity Competent Employees

	2/1/2005	4/1/2005	5/1/2005	6/1/2005	7/1/2005
Diversity Competent Employee (%)	5.5%	10.5%	13.8%	19.8%	27.3%
Diversity Competent Employee (%) Target	70.0%	70.0%	70.0%	70.0%	70.0%

Notes

Lorem ipsum dolor sit amet, consetetur sadipscing elitr, sed diam nonumy eirmod tempor invidunt ut labore et dolore magna aliquyam erat, sed diam voluptua. At vero eos et accusam et justo duo dolores et earebum. Stet clita kasd gubergren, no sea takimata sanctus est Lorem ipsum dolor sit amet. Lorem ipsum dolor sit amet, consetetur sadipscing elitr, sed diam nonumy

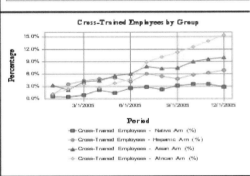

Cross-Trained Employees by Group

Cross-Trained Employees - Native Am (%)
Cross-Trained Employees - Hispanic Am (%)
Cross-Trained Employees - Asian Am (%)
Cross-Trained Employees - African Am (%)

Strategic Action Items

* Lorem ipsum dolor sit amet, consetetur sadipscing elitr, sed diam nonumy eirmod tempor invidunt ut

Source: Sample MetricLINK® Report

Building this type of technological competence frees the diversity professional up from some of the time-consuming yet critical tasks of tracking, calculating, and reporting a diversity initiative's results in bottom-line, performance-related terms.

The fundamental assumption is that all Diversity professionals need to keep abreast of the latest technology trends; thus, the selection and use of appropriate technologies is embedded into appropriate Diversity AOE knowledge areas. In this way technological competence is positioned as a valuable asset for all Diversity professionals as they strive for efficient execution of their AOE's. Indeed, such expertise will only become more important in the future.

Beyond Diversity Training and Learning Solutions

Some Diversity practitioners immediately think of Diversity Learning solutions when addressing diverse workplace performance issues since the Diversity profession has deep roots in the training field. Today, however, many Diversity professionals are expanding their scope to include solutions beyond the domain of traditional learning interventions. This trend is readily apparent when examining the Diversity AOE's that are likely to become more important in the next few years.

Diversity AOE's such as, Improving Organizational Performance, Measuring and Evaluating Diversity Impact, Facilitating Organizational Change does not always utilize learning as a primary solution. Roles such as Diversity Performance Technologist/Consultant and Diversity Business Partner will become mainstays for superior performance and contribution to the organization's effectiveness. An effective Diversity practitioner will need to master competencies in these areas to accurately perform a Diversity Return on Investment (DROI®) study. This is currently a "state-of-the-art" skill that will be mandatory and a source for competitive analysis and advantage in the near future.

Alignment for Performance and Success

Projected changes for the future confirm the evolution of the Diversity profession in this performance-driven, bottom-line direction and will influence how it is defined. The profession originated with a heavy emphasis on training to equip employees with the content knowledge and skills they needed to work with individuals across their differences and complexities. Now, the field has expanded to include utilizing the full context of diversity as a means to achieve not only individual results, but organization and business results as well.

More than ever before, organizations now expect Diversity professionals to truly understand the business and align all diversity performance improvement strategies and evaluation with overall business strategies in order to contribute to enhanced business results. Mastering the Diversity Areas of Expertise (DAOE's) reflected in this framework are prime requisite for meeting this challenge head on.

References

Bernthal, Paul R; Colteryahn, Karen; Davis, Patty, *et.al.*; *Mapping the Future: ASTD 2004 Competency Study*; Virginia, ASTD Press, 2004.

Bauer, I.; Heinl, R.; & McGovern, C.; (2003, June). Consultant Competency Model Role-based Analysis. Pittsburgh, PA. Development Dimensions International

Boyatzis, R., *The Competent Manager: A Model for Effective Performance.* New York: Wiley, 1982.

Brewster, C.; Farndale, E.; & van Ommeren, J.; (2000, June). "HR Competencies and Professional Standards." World Federation of Personnel Management Associations.

Hubbard, Edward E., *How to Calculate Diversity Return on Investment.* California: Global Insights Publishing, 1999.

Hubbard, Edward E., *The Diversity Scorecard.* Massachusetts: Butterworth-Heinemann, Elsevier Publishing, 2004.

Lewin, K., *Field Theory in Social Science.* New York: Harper, 1951.

Rothwell, W., "Strategic Needs Assessment." *Performance and Instruction Journal 23* (1984) 5: pp. 19-20.

Sredl, Henry J.; Rothwell, William J.; *Professional Training Roles and Competencies Volume I*, Massachusetts, HRD Press Inc., 1987.

Zemke, R., "Job Competencies: Can They Help You Design Better Training?" *Training 19* (1982) 5: pp. 28-31

CHAPTER 5

Diversity Discipline Competencies

Introduction

There have been many efforts to identify the roles of Diversity practitioners and the competencies associated with the successful performance of those roles. The goal of these efforts was to make the training of Diversity practitioners easier and increase the stature and credibility of Diversity as a formal profession.

As mentioned previously, the most fundamental element of a role, task or skill is a "competency." Competencies can be defined as the clusters of skills, knowledge, abilities and behaviors required for success in any job (Bernthal, Colteryahn, Davis, *et.al.*, 2004). A useful definition, widely accepted among human resource specialists in corporate environments, is "an underlying characteristic of a person which results in effective and/or superior performance on the job" (Klemp, 1980, p. 21). A more detailed definition, synthesized from the suggestions of several hundred experts in human resources development who attended a conference on the subject of competencies in Johannesburg in 1995, is "a cluster of related knowledge, skills, and attitudes that affects a major part of one's job (a role or responsibility), that correlates with performance on the job, that can be measured against well-accepted standards, and that can be improved via training and development" (Parry, 1996, p. 50).

The Complexities of Competencies

A competency model describes the particular combination of knowledge, skills, and characteristics needed to effectively perform a role in an organization and is used as a tool for selection, training and development, appraisal, and recognition. Although this might seem fairly straightforward, the more we consider what is entailed in identifying and measuring these competencies, the more complexities are revealed. Skills, for example, can range from highly concrete proficiencies, like the ability to operate a laptop computer or to write a sentence that clearly presents an idea, to far less tangible capabilities, such as the ability to think strategically or to influence others. Obviously any job requires a mixture of skills that may seem more or less measurable depending on their degree of concreteness. For example, devising a test to determine whether someone can type quickly and accurately enough to be a valuable member of a data gathering team is relatively easy. It is trickier to determine whether someone is skilled enough at strategic thinking and influencing others to be an effective Chief Diversity Officer.

Knowledge, too, can be either highly tangible and measurable—dc you know the proper procedures to conduct a cultural audit focus group?—or a far more complex matter: do you understand the workings of the Hispanic retail market and how it is likely to be affected by various global developments?

But of all the components involved, the characteristics of a person are probably the most complex and least readily measurable. A personal characteristic can be an aptitude, innate talent, or inclination that suggests a potential to acquire or use a particular kind of skill or knowledge. For example, a mathematical aptitude demonstrates a potential for acquiring statistical analysis skills. Other examples include a mechanical ability, a talent for logic, or an innate affinity for highly detailed work. Characteristics can also describe a personality trait that demonstrates a particular way of relating to the external environment. Personality traits such as self-confidence, self-sufficiency, or emotional stability may indicate a disposition for dealing with certain types of situations and performing certain kinds of diversity roles or functions. For example, self-sufficiency may suggest success in working independently with little supervision in a data analysis role.

Obviously, aptitude and basic personality traits are, to a certain extent, innate in an individual; you cannot teach an aptitude for mechanical things the way you can teach a particular rote skill. Still, someone with an aptitude for mechanical things is more able to master a mechanical process, just as someone with an aptitude for languages will be quicker to master German. However, as the second definition of competencies cited earlier indicates, a growing body of opinion says that even traits that might seem to be innate

dified and developed" (Zemke and Kramlinger, 1982,
ermore, even personality traits that might appear
quantifiable—charisma, for example—can be measured and
assessed when they are translated into behavioral terms.

The competency structure reflected in the Hubbard Diversity
Discipline Framework™ reveals both innate and acquired abilities.
It can be explained as essentially a pyramid (see Figure 5-1) built
on the foundation of inherent talents and incorporating the types
of skills and knowledge that can be acquired through learning,
effort, and experience. At the top of the pyramid is a specific
set of behaviors that are the manifestation of all the innate and
acquired abilities discussed earlier.

Figure 5-1:

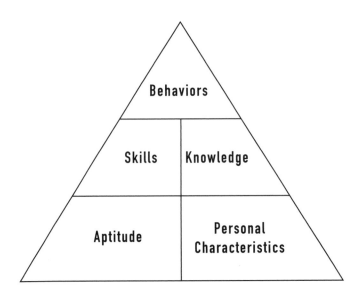

Source: The Art and Science of Competency Models by A. Lucia and
     R. Lepsinger, 1999

Expressing these abilities in behavioral terms is important for two reasons. First, for a competency model to be useful as a human resource tool, it must not only define the competencies necessary for effective performance but provide examples to illustrate when a particular competency is being demonstrated in a job. Second, although innate characteristics are fixed in a person for the most part, behaviors can be modified and taught. In other words, it might be difficult (some would say impossible) for a person lacking empathy to develop that trait, but empathetic behaviors, such as listening to customers' needs or addressing their concerns, can be fostered through training and development (Lucia, A. and Lepsinger, 1999).

Our data collection process for the development of the Hubbard Diversity Discipline Framework™ competency model consisted of interviews, questionnaires, focus groups, observation of high performers, and a combination of tools focused on concrete, specific behaviors that could be taught or altered through training, coaching, and other developmental approaches. Similarly, the Hubbard Diversity Discipline Framework™ model itself is couched in behavioral terms.

A Competency-based Diversity Approach that Reflects Value-Added Behaviors

The diversity competencies shown in the Hubbard Diversity Discipline Framework™ are extremely useful in the day-to-day resolution of diversity-related issues and concerns. They have proven to be vital for the effective, credible delivery of value-

ions to organizations. (See Figure 5-2 and Figure 5-3)

STRATEGIC DIVERSITY COMPETENCIES
- ▶ Diversity Knowledge and Skills Competencies
- ▶ Technical Competencies
- ▶ Business Competencies
- ▶ Interpersonal Competencies
- ▶ Intellectual Competencies
- ▶ Personal Competencies

These diversity competencies are designed to help identify and build the essential skills, knowledge, and personal characteristics needed for successful performance as a diversity professional. Each competency cluster is defined and the competencies within the cluster are described here in detail.

Figure 5-3:

Cluster One: Diversity Knowledge and Skills Competencies:

Having knowledge and skills related to diversity concepts, theories, strategies, tools and techniques, and their application to organizational objectives and results.

▶ **Diversity Concepts, Theories, and Understanding**
  – Knowing the key concepts and variables, such as national and workforce demographics, EEO versus Affirmative

Action versus Diversity, multiple perspectives covering issues of bias, stereotyping, prejudice, institutionalized "isms;" able to identify fundamental research, approaches, and underpinnings upon which the diversity field is based. This requires knowledge of the origins and history of diversity and diverse group issues and their impact; understanding of legal and legislative issues; understanding current and future socioeconomic trends; knowledge of language and terminology of diversity and inclusion; knowledge of race relations; awareness of institutional barriers.

▶ **Cultural Sensitivity Impact and Understanding** – Knowing what is appropriate cultural protocol, values, beliefs, behavior, and nuances that are required for effective interpersonal communication and process; knowledge of the field and the literature of specific cultural groups; knowledge of cultural, intercultural, and racial phenomena; understanding of the implications of language differences; knowledge of culture—one's own and others'; receptiveness and appreciation of differences, ambiguity, and uncertainty; openness to new experiences and people.

▶ **Micro-inequities Sensitivity Analysis Skill** – Assessing gradational differences in situational and behavioral treatment among and between groups that result in a discriminatory impact. Ability to assess whether equitable standards of care regarding individual and group treatment are met and if disparate impact and/or internalized oppression has occurred as a result of such treatment.

▶ **Diversity and Business Linkages** – Defining the business rationale for diversity, communicating the business rationale for diversity; aligning diversity and strategic business objectives; identifying aspects and elements of diversity in operational work processes; educating and showing others connections between diversity and business requirements.

▶ **Diversity Measurement Skill** – Identifying quantitative calculations, qualitative observations, and anecdotal descriptions of diversity impact; assessing alternatives in terms of their financial, psychological, and strategic advantages and disadvantages. Requires tools for identifying direct and indirect costs, judging probability, and weighing trade-offs; scanning, synthesizing, and drawing conclusions from diversity data.

▶ **Diversity ROI Measurement Skill** – Using Hubbard Diversity ROI Model™ and DROI® quantitative calculations, qualitative observations, and anecdotal descriptions of diversity impact; assessing alternatives in terms of their ROI trade-offs and financial impact, forecasting diversity return-on-investment impact, and drawing conclusions from the financial data.

▶ **Diversity Strategy and Model Building Skill** – Conceptualizing and developing theoretical and practical diversity frameworks and business plan strategies for business alignment, and applying implementation and integration skills.

► **Gender Behavior Impact and Understanding** –
Knowing key concepts, theories, gender-based difference
models and the perceptions of roles related to gender in
the workplace and community that can affect individual
and group contributions; assessing impact of gender-
based treatment on culture and performance; knowledge
of the implications of the women's movement; knowledge
of emerging work in the white male diversity movement;
knowledge of policy and practices for achieving equality
in the workplace; awareness of the nature of gender bias
and its impact; awareness of gender development theories;
ability to facilitate sometimes volatile gender based group
discussions; knowledge of the nature and role of gender in
work-family initiatives.

► **People with Disabilities Sensitivities and
Understanding** – Self knowledge of attitudes, beliefs
and prejudices regarding people with disabilities and how
these attitudes, beliefs, and prejudices influence behavior;
the ability to exhibit favorable attitudes toward people
with disabilities and to appreciate their contributions;
recognition that persons with disabilities are whole persons
with a broad range of abilities and potential for growth
and development; understanding historical treatment,
social perceptions, and language related to persons with
disabilities; ability to communicate respect for persons with
disabilities by use of appropriate language, behaviors, and
interventions; ability to respect personal boundaries in
conversations with and inquires of persons with disabilities;
current knowledge of laws and policies regarding people

with disabilities; ability to act in compliance with the ADA and other relevant legislation and policy; ability to select intervention approaches relevant to the culture, values, and lifestyles of the client; knowledge of the facts about particular disabilities and ability to differentiate myth from reality regarding limitations; ability to recognize workplace issues and to act to create a positive supportive environment; ability to provide opportunities for advancement and supportive feedback in the workplace for people with disabilities.

▶ **Sexual Orientation, Transsexual, and Transgender Sensitivities and Understanding** – Having an awareness of the definitional differences between the meanings of sexual orientation, transsexual, transgender, gay, lesbian, bisexual and transvestite; the ability to discuss issues of sexual orientation and sexuality openly as a means of beginning to deal constructively with homophobia; the ability to create a variety of learning opportunities that allow people to go beyond awareness to address their own issues of homophobia; the ability to facilitate the process by which lesbians, gay men, bisexuals, and transgender people can be fully incorporated into organizations as fully functioning and acknowledged human beings; a basic understanding of the legal rights of gays and lesbians, in order to be credible when responding to questions and working with individuals who have experienced homophobia and sexual orientation discrimination.

► **World/Global View** – Conceptualizing and analyzing situations with global lenses to bring a world or global context for addressing diverse workforce and other situations; knowing how to effectively use country-specific protocol to interact with others from different locations and countries.

Cluster Two: Technical Competencies:
Having functional skills and knowledge to perform a diversity related role or task.

► **Competency Identification** – Identifying the knowledge, skill and attitudinal requirements of jobs, tasks and roles required for individual and business performance; requires skill in identifying inputs, processes, outputs, and assessing their accuracy and completeness to affect outcomes.

► **Objectives Preparation** – Preparing clear statements that describe desired outputs; requires skill in identifying relevant outputs and proposing criteria to measure their attainment.

► **Performance Observation** – Tracking and describing behaviors and their effects; requires skill in identifying what drives or causes behaviors.

► **Written Communication** – The ability to express oneself clearly in business writing.

Cluster Three: Business Competencies:
Having a strong management, economic, or administration base.

▶ **Analyzing Needs and Proposing Solutions** – Identifying and understanding business issues and client needs, problems and opportunities comparing data from different sources to draw conclusions; using effective approaches for choosing a course of action or developing appropriate solutions; taking action that is consistent with available facts, constraints and probable consequences.

▶ **Applying Business Understanding** – Knowing how the functions of a business work and relate to one another; knowing the economic impact of business decisions; requires the ability to use tools for identifying how business functions interrelate and the economic impact of those relationships. Understanding the organization's business model and financial goals; utilizing economic, financial, and organizational data to build and document the business case for investing in workplace diversity and performance solutions; using business terminology when communicating to others.

▶ **Cost-benefit Analysis** – Assessing alternatives in terms of their financial, psychological, and strategic advantages and disadvantages; requires ability to utilize tools for identifying direct and indirect costs, judging probability, and weighing trade-offs.

▶ **Driving Results** – Identifying opportunities for

improvement and setting well-defined goals related to workplace diversity and performance solutions; orchestrating efforts and measuring progress; striving to achieve goals and produce exceptional results.

▶ **Industry Understanding** – Knowing the key concepts and variables, such as critical issues, economic vulnerabilities, measurements, distribution channels, inputs, outputs, and information sources, that defines an industry or section.

▶ **Organizational Behavior Understanding** – Seeing organizations as dynamic, political, economic, and social systems that have multiple goals; using this larger framework for understanding and influencing events and change; requires skills to utilize organizational models and tools for describing the system components and how they interplay.

▶ **Organizational Development Theories and Techniques Understanding** – Knowing the techniques and methods used in organizational development, effectiveness, and understanding their appropriate use; ability to use organization development models, processes, and methods.

▶ **Organizational Understanding** – Knowing the strategy, structure, power networks, financial position and systems of a specific organization; developing skill in gaining access to organizational information and interpreting that information.

▶ **Thinking Strategically** – Understanding internal and external factors that affect workplace diversity and performance in organizations, keeping abreast of trends and anticipating opportunities to add value to the business or organization; operating from a systems perspective in developing workplace diversity and performance strategies and building alignment with business strategies.

▶ **Planning and Implementing Assignments** – Developing action plans, obtaining resources, and completing assignments in a timely manner to ensure that workplace diversity and performance goals are achieved.

▶ **Business Integration Skill** – The ability to systematically design, incorporate, and help implement elements of diversity differences, similarities and strategies into the fabric of an organization's processes and systems.

▶ **Change Management Leadership** – The ability to demonstrate support for innovation and for organizational changes needed to improve the organization's effectiveness; initiating, sponsoring, and implementing organizational change; helping others to successfully manage the structural process dynamics and the behavioral process dynamics of organizational change.

▶ **Customer Intimacy Skill** – A deep and detailed knowledge of customer cultural norms and buying habits. The ability to match customer product needs by demographic segment; systematic increases in market penetration and share of wallet; up-to-date data and intelligence on key target and multiethnic market segments; customer satisfaction maintenance and improvement; and trust and relationship building for the long-term.

Cluster Four: Interpersonal Competencies:
Having a strong communication and rapport-building skills.

▶ **Feedback and Reporting Skill** – Communicating information, opinions, observations, and conclusions so that they are understood and can be acted upon.

▶ **Networking and Partnering Skill** – Developing and using a network of collaborative relationships with internal and external contacts to leverage the differences and similarities of individuals as well as any diversity-focused strategies derived to facilitate the accomplishment of business and/or organizational results

▶ **Group Process Skill** – Influencing groups so that tasks, relationships, and individual needs are addressed requires the use of tools to create exercises in knowing, learning, and application; knowledge of adult education methods such as simulations and role plays or experiential learning; knowledge of group dynamics and intervention strategies.

▶ **Negotiation Skill** – Securing win-win agreements while successfully representing a special interest in a decision-making process; conflict resolution skills; ability to deal with defensiveness, hostility, anger and resistance.

▶ **Building Trust and Rapport** – Interacting across individual and situational differences in a way that gives others confidence in your intentions and those of the organization.

▶ **Questioning** – Gathering information by stimulating insight in individuals and groups through the use of interviews, questionnaires, and other probing methods that reveal information that is relevant and leads to insight.

▶ **Relationship Building Across Differences and Complexities** – Establishing relationships and networks across a broad range of people, groups and situations requires skill and methods to sort relevant from irrelevant cultural nuances and select appropriate behavior. Utilizing diversity awareness and skills in a way that facilitates the accomplishment of business results.

▶ **Communicating Effectively Across Cultures** – Expressing thoughts, feelings and ideas in a clear, concise and compelling manner in both individual and diverse group situations; actively listening to others; adjusting your style to capture the attention of your diverse audience; developing and deploying targeted communications strategies that inform and build support across a diverse audience.

▶ **Influencing Stakeholders** – Selling the value of diversity and inclusion or a recommended solution as a way of improving organizational performance; gaining commitment to solutions that will improve individual, team and organizational performance.

Cluster Five: Intellectual Competencies:
Having knowledge and skill related to thinking and information processing

▶ **Data Reduction Skill** – Scanning, synthesizing, and drawing conclusions from data.

▶ **Information Search Skill** – Gathering information from printed and other recorded sources; identifying and using information specialists and reference services and aids.

▶ **Intellectual Versatility** – Recognizing, exploring, and using a broad range of ideas and practices; thinking logically and creatively without undue influence from personal biases; cognitive and behavioral flexibility.

▶ **Model-Building Skill** – Conceptualizing and developing theoretical and practical frameworks that describe complete ideas in understandable, usable ways; ability to use a systemic approach.

▶ **Observing Skill** – Recognizing objectively what is happening in and across situations.

▶ **Visioning Skill** – Projecting trends and visualizing possible and probable futures and their implications.

Cluster Six: Personal Competencies:

Having skills to successfully interact with people and/or situations that may be different by modifying your behavior to meet the needs of a person(s) or situation.

▶ **Demonstrating Adaptability** – Maintaining effectiveness when working with others who are different from you in abilities, motivations, backgrounds, cultures, *etc.*; remaining open to new people, thoughts, and approaches; adjusting effectively to work within new work structures, processes, requirements, or cultures; willingness and ability to withstand pressures such as another person's discomfort, discontent, and negative reactions; ability to renew oneself and prevent burnout.

▶ **Diversity Orientation** – Seek out and build relationships with people who are different than yourself in race, gender, ethnicity, physical ability, sexual orientation, age, *etc*; learn about differences in the workforce through reading, attending workshops, fostering relationships with people who are different, and participating in activities that are diversity related. Actively identifying new areas for one's own personal diversity learning; regularly creating and taking advantage of cultural and other learning opportunities; applying the newly gained knowledge and skill.

▶ **Champion for Diversity** – Demonstrate a zero-tolerance policy towards any type of discrimination (age, race, sex, class, sexual orientation, physical ability, *etc*); personally communicate support for diversity internally and externally using all media and available channels.

▶ **Personal Credibility** – Demonstrated ability to be perceived as responsible, reliable, and trustworthy; ability to examine one's own baggage; demonstrates authenticity, self-disclosure, forgiveness, integrity, and empathy; is ethical.

▶ **Leadership Skill** – Taking actions to challenge processes and ideas to improve and/or innovate current direction; inspires a shared vision among individuals and groups; empowers others to act; models the way through personal actions taken; encourages the heart of individuals and groups; inspires commitment, persistence and involvement. This also requires skillful use of personal and organizational change strategies and methods; demonstrates courage.

Benefits of Using a Competency-based Approach

To better understand the benefits of a competency-based diversity framework system, picture this scenario: you are able to hire people who have high potential to succeed as a diversity professional, to ensure that they receive the training and development necessary to realize that potential, and to provide an appraisal system that gives them the feedback and coaching they need to perform well. Imagine also being able to focus on the skills, knowledge, and characteristics they need and to ensure that they understand what it takes to grow as an effective, well respected practitioner. And finally, envision being able to demonstrate that the behaviors and skills you identify and develop are proven predictors of success. How can you do all this? By identifying the traits that contribute to the success of the profession's top performers.

The Hubbard Diversity Measurement and Productivity Institute staff is completing a project of this nature. It is the framework upon which this book and competencies are based. In future books, we will detail specific training and development programs and practices that help practitioners gain the knowledge, skills abilities and attitudes needed to perform these roles, areas of expertise and competencies.

References

ASTD, *Elements of Competence for Diversity Work: Creating Competence for Inclusive Work Environments*, Alexandria, Virginia. ASTD Press, 1996.

Bernthal, Paul R; Colteryahn, Karen; Davis, Patty, *et.al.*; *Mapping the Future: ASTD 2004 Competency Study*; Virginia, ASTD Press, 2004.

Hubbard, Edward E., *How to Calculate Diversity Return on Investment.* California: Global Insights Publishing, 1999.

Hubbard, Edward E., *The Diversity Scorecard.* Massachusetts: Butterworth-Heinemann, Elsevier Publishing, 2004.

Klemp, G. O., (Ed) *The Assessment of Occupational Competence.* Washington, D.C.: Report to the National Institute of Education, 1980.

Lucia, A., and Lepsinger, R., *The Art and Science of Competency Models.* San Francisco, California, Jossey-Bass, 1999.

Sredl, Henry J.; Rothwell, William J.; *Professional Training Roles and Competencies Volume I*, Massachusetts, HRD Press Inc., 1987.

Zemke, R., and Kramlinger, T., *Figuring Things Out: A Trainer's Guide to Needs and Task Analysis.* Reading, Mass.: Addison-Wesley, 1982.

CHAPTER 6

Diversity Measurement & Diversity Return On Investment (DROI®)

Introduction

If the Diversity profession is to be treated as a well-defined, serious discipline, then diversity analytics and measurement protocols must be a common place part of its landscape. Although interest in measuring the effects of diversity has been growing, the topic still challenges even the most sophisticated and progressive diversity organizations. Diversity professionals and managers know they must begin to show how diversity is linked to the bottom-line in hard numbers or they will have difficulty maintaining funding, gaining support, and assessing progress. In short, they must calculate and report their ***diversity return-on-investment*** **(DROI®)**.

Diversity executives and professionals must be able to effectively address critical issues such as:

will we be able to demonstrate that diversity contributes to the organization's bottom line?

▶ How do we show senior executives and others that diversity is a strategic business partner that is aligned and linked to the strategic goals and objectives of the organization?

▶ How can we measure the impact of diversity on organizational performance and an improved work environment?

▶ How does the strategic diversity process help an organization excel in the domestic and global marketplace and provide favorable returns to stockholders and stakeholders?

If your organization is like most, you have probably found it challenging to answer these questions. Experience has shown that the diversity organization has its own brand of strategy and visions and has developed its own perspective regarding the value of its efforts to implement a diverse work environment; however, senior leaders and line management are skeptical, at best, of diversity's impact on the organization's success and their ability to demonstrate any financial or strategic contributions that a diverse workforce makes to the bottom line. In many firms, executives and others want to believe the cliché that views people as the organization's most important asset; however, they simply cannot understand how diversity realistically makes that vision a reality that results in a measurable difference in organizational performance.

Organizations typically define their diversity efforts in terms of race and gender, which get reflected in the elements they track regularly. This list is usually sorted by demographic group and might include items such as number recruited, employee turnover, cost per hire, number of minority personnel or women on the organization's board of directors, and employee attitudes. Now consider those diversity attributes that push beyond race and gender that you believe are crucial to implementing your organization's competitive strategy. In this list, you might include items such as penetrating diverse customer markets, retaining capable and committed diverse work teams that generate new, paradigm-shifting ideas in half the time of competitors, improving customer issue resolution processes, reducing cycle time, increasing market share and shareholder value, and the like.

How well do your existing diversity measures capture the strategic diversity drivers you identified in the second list? For most organizations, there will not be a very close match between the two lists. Even more important, in those firms where diversity professionals think there is a close match, the senior executives frequently do not agree that this second list actually describes how diversity creates value. In either case, a serious disconnect exists between what is measured and what is important to organizational performance.

These questions are fundamental because new economic realities are putting pressure on organizations to widen their traditional focus of diversity as the guardian of ethnic representation and social well-being to a broader, more strategic factor in business success. As a primary source of production and

pact, our economy has shifted from physical
ital (which comes in all colors, backgrounds,
ns, thinking styles, and so on). As a result,
sity managers are increasingly coming under fire
emonstrate exactly how they are helping the organization
organize, utilize, and document this critically significant
organizational asset to create performance and value.

The primary issue that diversity must deal with is difficult for some
to imagine and believe (*i.e.*, showing diversity's measurable impact
on organizational strategy and the financial bottom line). The
ability to utilize a diverse mixture of human and other resources
to create a unique blend of strategy-focused solutions, by its very
nature, creates an innovative competitive process that is difficult to
copy—thus making it a competitive advantage (largely invisible to
competitors).

Simply put, utilizing diversity as a strategic asset keeps an
organization's competitive edge sharp for the long haul. This
makes diversity a prime source of sustainable competitive
potential. To realize this potential, however, diversity professionals
must understand the organization's strategic plan for developing
and sustaining this competitive advantage throughout the
organization and its marketplace. In order to gain its benefits, this
diversity must be utilized.

Before we discuss diversity analytics and how to measure and
calculate diversity's return on investment (DROI®), we should
define what we mean when we use the term "diversity."

What do we mean when we say "diversity"?

As mentioned earlier, according to Dr. Roosevelt Thomas, "Diversity" can be defined as a collective mixture characterized by differences and similarities that are applied in pursuit of organizational objectives (Thomas, 1996, 1999). This definition highlights that diversity is about **both** differences and similarities and their application in the context of the organization. From a diversity measurement standpoint, it suggests that it is the *utilization* of these mixtures in the context of the organization that creates an opportunity to measure diversity's impact. Therefore, I define "Diversity Management" as the process of planning for, organizing, directing, and supporting these collective mixtures in a way that adds a measurable difference to organizational performance (Hubbard, 1999, 2004).

From an analysis standpoint, Diversity can be organized into four interdependent and sometimes overlapping aspects: Workforce Diversity, Behavioral Diversity, Structural Diversity, and Business and Global Diversity.

Workforce Diversity encompasses group and situational identities of the organization's employees (*i.e.*, gender, race, ethnicity, religion, sexual orientation, physical ability, age, family status, economic background and status, and geographical background and status). It also includes changes in the labor market demographics.

Behavioral Diversity encompasses work styles, thinking styles, learning styles, communication styles, aspirations, beliefs/value system, as well as changes in employees' attitudes and expectations.

Structural Diversity encompasses interactions across functions, across organizational levels in the hierarchy, across divisions and between parent companies and subsidiaries, and across organizations engaged in strategic alliances and cooperative ventures. As organizations attempt to become more flexible, less layered, more team-based, and more multi- and cross-functional, measuring this type of diversity will be essential.

Business and Global Diversity encompasses the expansion and segmentation of customer markets, the diversification of products and services offered, and the variety of operating environments in which organizations work and compete (*i.e.*, legal and regulatory context, labor market realities, community and societal expectations/relationships, business cultures and norms). Increasing competitive pressures, globalization, rapid advances in product technologies, changing demographics in the customer bases both within domestic markets and across borders, and shifts in business/government relationships all signal a need to measure an organization's response and impact on business diversity.

What sites must be visited along the measurement journey?

Calculating diversity's return-on-investment requires asking key questions and performing key tasks along the way. To achieve a successful result, measuring diversity return-on-investment (DROI®) requires a systematic approach that takes into account both costs and benefits. The Hubbard Diversity ROI Analysis Model provides a step-by-step approach that keeps the process manageable such that diversity practitioners can tackle one issue at a time.

Hubbard Diversity ROI Analysis Model™

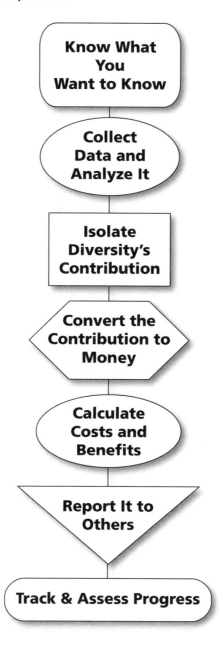

Diversity as a full-fledged discipline should contain models that lead a diversity professional through a holistic application of processes for success. The DROI® Model easily meets that requirement. The model emphasizes a logical, systematic process, which flows from one step to another. Applying the model provides consistency from one DROI® calculation to another. In essence, it suggests that the major aspects of diversity measurement you need to address to calculate diversity's ROI impact include:

▶ Knowing what you want to know

▶ Collecting data and analyzing it

▶ Isolating diversity's contribution

▶ Converting the contribution to money

▶ Calculating the costs and benefits

▶ Reporting it to others

▶ Tracking and assessing progress

Step 1: Know What You Want To Know

Conducting a diversity return-on-investment study requires that you clearly identify what you want to know as a result of implementing the study. This should be based upon, at bare minimum, the identification of a business problem or opportunity related to the organization's key business strategy. Second, you should be prepared to list a series of research questions you would like answered or hypotheses you would like to test. These questions may include things such as "In what racial categories do we have the most turnover?", "What diverse customer markets are not utilizing our products or services?", "How can we improve the idea and solution generation (creative) process using current cross-functional teams to improve operational performance?", *etc.*

While planning ways to address these research questions and ideas, it may be helpful to begin with the end in mind. That is, think of what will appear on your research report, create placeholders for them, and then generate the questions or hypotheses that must be answered in order for data to show up on the report as results. The final step in this phase is to summarize the questions you would like answered and formulate diversity measurement study objectives that will guide your work. Once this is done, you are ready to consider the appropriate data collection methods and develop your data collection plan.

Step 2: Collect Data And Analyze It

Data collection is central to the diversity return-on-investment (DROI®) process. In some situations, post-DROI® study data are collected and compared to pre-study situations, control group differences, and expectations. Both hard data, representing output, quality, cost, time and frequency; and soft data, including work habits, work climate, and attitudes are collected. Data are collected using a variety of methods including but not limited to:

▶ Follow-up surveys

- ▶ Post-study interviews

- ▶ Focus groups

- ▶ Short term pilot project assignments

- ▶ Action plans

- ▶ Performance contracts (agreements to produce certain levels of results)

- ▶ Performance monitoring (reports and other literature reviews)

- ▶ *Etc.*

The important challenge in the data collection phase is to select the method or methods appropriate for the organizational setting and within the time and budget constraints of the organization. During this phase, you will identify the data collection processes and specific metrics to use, create the appropriate evaluation instruments, and apply an organizational change methodology such as the Hubbard Diversity 9-S Framework (Shared Vision, Shared Values, Standards, Strategy, Structure, Systems, Style, Skills and Staff).

Step 3: Isolate Diversity's Contribution

An often-overlooked issue in most diversity assessments or evaluation studies is the process of isolating the effects of diversity.

In this step of the process, specific strategies are explored, which determine the amount of output performance directly related to the diversity initiative. This step is essential because there are many factors that will influence performance data after the diversity initiative. The result is increased accuracy and credibility of the DROI® calculation. The following strategies have been utilized by organizations to tackle this important issue:

▶ Control groups

▶ Trend line analyses

▶ Forecasting model

▶ Participant estimates

▶ Supervisor of participant estimates

▶ Senior management estimates

▶ Expert estimates

▶ Subordinate's estimates (those who work for the participants)

▶ Identifying other influencing factors

▶ Customer inputs

Collectively, these strategies provide a comprehensive set of tools to tackle the important and critical issue of isolating the effects of diversity initiatives.

Calculating and isolating diversity's return-on-investment will require an analysis of operational and other business processes to isolate the specific areas where diversity can be applied to improve business performance. One tool to analyze operational processes is the "S-I-P-O-C Chain." This analysis tool allows you to break down operational processes and view them in terms of the way business is done from *Supplier* to *Input* to *Process* to *Output* to *Customer*. Once all contributing factors have been identified and their contributions calculated you would be ready to convert the contribution to money.

Step 4: Convert The Contribution To Money

To calculate the diversity return-on-investment, data collected in a DROI® evaluation study are converted to monetary values and are compared to the diversity initiative costs. This requires a value to be placed on each unit of data connected with the initiative. There are at least ten different strategies available to convert data to monetary values. The specific strategy selected usually depends on the type of data and the initiative under analysis:

- ▶ **Output data** are converted to profit contribution or cost saving. In this strategy, output increases are converted to monetary value based on their unit contribution to profit or the unit of cost reduction.

- ▶ The **cost of quality** is calculated and quality improvements are directly converted to cost savings.

- ▶ For diversity initiatives where employee time is saved, the

participant's wages and benefits are used for the value of time. Because a variety of programs focus on improving the time required to complete projects, processes, or daily activities, the value of time becomes an important and critical issue.

► **Historical costs** are used when they are available for a specific variable. In this case, organizational cost data are utilized to establish the specific value of an improvement.

► When available, **internal and external experts** may be used to estimate a value for an improvement. In this situation, the credibility of the estimate hinges on the expertise and reputation of the individual.

► **External databases** are sometimes available to estimate the value or cost of data items. Research, government, and industry databases can provide important information for these values. The difficulty lies in finding a specific database related to the diversity initiative under analysis.

► **Participants** estimate the value of the data item. For this approach to be effective, participants must be capable of providing a value for the improvement.

► **Supervisors of participants** provide estimates when they are both willing and capable of assigning values to the improvement. This approach is especially useful when participants are not fully capable of providing this input or in situations where supervisors need to confirm or adjust the participant's estimate.

- **Senior management** may provide estimates on the values of an improvement. This approach is particularly helpful to establish values for performance measures that are very important to senior management.

- **Diversity staff** estimates may be used to determine a value of an output data item. In these cases, it is essential for the estimates to be provided on an unbiased basis.

Step 4 in the Hubbard Diversity Return-on-investment Analysis Model is very important and is absolutely necessary for determining the monetary benefits from a diversity initiative. The process is challenging, particularly with soft data, but can be methodologically accomplished using one or more of these strategies.

Step 5: Calculate the Costs and Benefits

Calculating the Diversity Initiative Costs

To successfully calculate DROI®, both cost and benefits must be tracked and calculated in the process. The first part of the equation on a cost/benefit analysis is the diversity initiative costs. Tabulating the costs involves monitoring or developing all of the related costs of the diversity initiative targeted for the DROI® calculation. Among the cost components that should be included are:

- The cost to design and develop the diversity initiative, possibly prorated over the expected life of the initiative;

- ▶ The cost of any materials and external staff resources utilized;

- ▶ The costs of any facilities travel, lodging, *etc.*

- ▶ Salaries, plus employee benefits of the employee's involved;

- ▶ Administrative and overhead costs allocated in some way.

Calculating the Diversity Return on Investment

The diversity return-on-investment is calculated using the initiative's benefits and costs. The benefit/cost ratio (BCR) is the initiative benefits divided by cost. In formula form it is:

BCR = Diversity Initiative Benefits / Diversity Initiative Costs

Sometimes the ratio is stated as a cost-to-benefit ratio, although the formula is the same as BCR.

The diversity return on investment calculation uses the net benefits of the diversity initiative divided by the initiative costs. The net benefits are the diversity initiative benefits minus the costs. As a formula, it is stated as:

DROI®% = (Net Diversity Initiative Benefits / Initiative Costs)*100

In other words, the DROI® formula is calculated as:

((Diversity Benefits – Initiative Costs) / Initiative Cost) x 100

This is the same basic formula used in evaluating other investments where the ROI is traditionally reported as earnings divided by investment. The DROI® from some diversity initiatives is often high. DROI® figures above 450% are not uncommon.

Identifying Intangible Benefits

In addition to tangible, monetary benefits, most diversity initiatives will have intangible, non-monetary benefits. The DROI® calculation is based on converting both hard and soft data to monetary values. Intangible benefits include items such as:

► Increased job satisfaction

► Increased organizational commitment

► Improved teamwork

► Reduced conflict

► *Etc.*

During data analysis, every attempt is made to convert all data to monetary values. All hard data such as output, quality, and time are converted to monetary values. The conversion of soft data is attempted for each data item. However, if the process used for conversion is too subjective or inaccurate, the resulting values can lose credibility in the process. This data should be listed as an intangible benefit with the appropriate explanation. For some diversity initiatives, intangible, non-monetary benefits are extremely valuable, often carrying as much influence as the hard data items.

Step 6: Report It to Others

Next, it is critical that you have an organized communications plan to let others know the progress and challenges being addressed by diversity initiatives. During the development cycle of the communications plan, it is important to identify communication vehicles to use, how and when the report will be created, when it will be delivered and how to evaluate its implementation.

Step 7: Track and Assess Progress

Finally, in order to maintain any gains made or benefits from lessons learned during the process, you must make plans to track and assess the effectiveness of your diversity initiatives over time.

Your Challenge

The skills to implement a diversity return-on-investment study are critical to the success of the organization and the credibility and survival of the diversity profession. In order to be taken seriously as a profession, diversity practitioners must become adept at measuring diversity results that tie diversity to the organization's bottom-line objectives. By using a systematic, logical, planned approach, the diversity return-on-investment process is one of the diversity practitioner's best tools to demonstrate improved performance and diversity's contribution to the bottom-line!

References:

Hubbard, Edward E., *How to Calculate Diversity Return on Investment*. Petaluma, CA: Global Insights, 1999.

Hubbard, Edward E., *The Diversity Scorecard*. London: Butterworth Heinemann-Elsever, 2004.

Hubbard, Edward E., *The Manager's Pocket Guide to Diversity Management*. Burlington, MA: HRD Press, 2004.

Thomas, R. Roosevelt, Jr., *Building a House for Diversity*. New York: AMACOM, 1999.

Thomas, R. Roosevelt, Jr., *Redefining Diversity*. New York: AMACOM, 1996.

CHAPTER 7

The Hubbard Five-Level Diversity Measurement Taxonomy

Introduction

Diversity measurement is one of several activities that must be undertaken to add more rigor and substance to diversity as a credible profession. The only way to determine if a diversity intervention is having the desired effect is to use a formal diversity measurement taxonomy which helps to categorize the level of measurement sophistication being utilized. The results of these activities can confirm the level of impact of a diversity initiative and identify the range of growth and improvements that are possible. Implementing a diversity measurement strategy for evaluation can contribute to maximizing the organization's return on investment and highlight progress and growth.

The reason I developed this five-level diversity measurement taxonomy for the diversity discipline was to clarify the operating

levels of a diversity intervention and to further define
.ng of "diversity levels of evaluation." Some organizations
.pport diversity practitioner's work at a "compliance" level
.cerned primarily with meeting EEO and Affirmative Action
.equirements. Others operate at a much higher "strategic" level
using applications demonstrating an advanced level of commitment
and characterized by the integration and measurement of diversity
initiatives for their strategic impact on identified business needs.
However, they are both connected along a continuum that offers
degrees of value at each level up to and including return on
investment.

These five levels are important and must be understood by all
diversity practitioners and professionals in the field. The Hubbard
diversity five-level taxonomy represents a sequence of ways to
evaluate a diversity intervention or aspects of the diversity change
process. As you move from one level to the next, the process
becomes more difficult and time intensive, yet provides more
valuable information. None of the levels should be by-passed
since each level contributes to the strategic, holistic nature of the
intervention. Professionals applying the Diversity Discipline would
categorize their measurement interventions using the following
levels:

- ▶ Level 1: Activities Focused Level or Intangibles

- ▶ Level 2: Compliance

- ▶ Level 3: Inclusion

- ▶ Level 4: Strategic Performance

- ▶ Level 5: Profit-Focused ROI Level and
  Mission Focused ROI Level

Figure: 7-1

Hubbard Diversity Metrics Taxonomy™	
Level	**Description**
Level 1: Activities Focused Level (Intangibles)	Diversity metric applications that highlight positive results that either cannot be converted to monetary values or would involve too much time or expense in the conversion to be worth the effort. The range of intangible outcomes is practically limitless.
	It is important to note that, even though any of the intangible benefits may not be converted in one evaluation study, they may be converted in another study or in another organization. Not all measures can or should be converted to monetary values. By design, some should be captured and reported as intangible measures. Although they may not be perceived as valuable as the measures converted to monetary values, as stated earlier, intangible measures are critical to the overall evaluation process.
Level 2: Compliance	Diversity metric applications "demonstrating a weak to moderate commitment to increasing minority representation within the organization." It presupposes cursory attention to diversity in compliance with EEO and Affirmative Action laws or concern with "representation level" mixtures of diverse people in the organization. Compliance level metrics foster a focus on diversity measurement to help assess the impact of the organization's diverse workforce recruiting and retention efforts. However, they tend to be limited to assuring the organization has met its Affirmative Action and/or EEO requirements. Organizations operating at this level are often only interested in whether diversity in the workforce is present in denominations that equal the Civilian Labor Force (CLF) or other representational benchmarks. Diversity metrics at this level are not often used to drive business or mission performance.

Figure: 7-1 continued:

Hubbard Diversity Metrics Taxonomy™	
Level	**Description**
Level 3: Inclusion	Diversity metric applications involving a higher level of commitment to diversity activities, accompanied by the strong support of senior management and the development of programs designed to build a diversity-friendly environment. It also includes building a diversity focused infrastructure to take advantage its diverse talent and capability. It is also important that the definition of diversity at this stage and its associated metrics are broad and inclusive, capturing all employee segments – gender, race, ethnicity, religion, sexual orientation, disability, *etc.* This helps move the diversity process from a "basic" stage to an "improved capability" stage that promotes full utilization of all people.
Level 4: Strategic Performance	Diversity metric applications demonstrating an advanced level of commitment and characterized by the integration and measurement of diversity initiatives for their strategic impact on identified business needs. It also includes the strategic use of formal scorecards and diversity focused bonus and incentive plans to create measurable change in the organization's performance. This helps move the diversity process from a "proactive" stage to building "strategic capability."

Figure: 7-1 continued:

Hubbard Diversity Metrics Taxonomy™	
Level	**Description**
Level 5: Diversity Return On Investment (DROI)	Diversity metric applications measuring the anticipated profitability of a diversity initiative investment. It is used as a means to measure the performance of an organization's application of diversity in financial terms. The investment portion of the formula represents capital expenditures such as a training facilities or equipment plus initial development or production costs. The original investment figure can be used or production costs, or the present book value can be expressed as the average investment over a period of time. If the diversity program is a one-time offering, then the figure is the original investment. However, if the initial costs are spread over a period of time, then the average book value is usually more appropriate. This value is essentially half the initial costs since, through depreciation, a certain fixed part of investment is written off each year over the life of the investment.

Note! The last four levels of evaluation build in sequence. That is, in order to assess that your organization's diversity measurement processes are operating at the next highest level, your metrics must include all of the metric levels below it. For example, if you feel that your diversity metrics operate at the Strategic performance level, the organization must fully utilize metrics at the Compliance and Inclusion levels.

Let's take a closer look at each of these levels in more detail.

Activity-Level or Intangibles

Most successful diversity initiatives result in some intangible benefits. Activity or intangible (anecdotal) benefits should be measured and reported since they are often the first level of movement towards an objective. They can be used as additional evidence of a diversity initiative's success and can be presented as supportive qualitative data. Activity or intangibles may not carry the weight of measures that are expressed in dollars and cents, but they are still a very important part of the overall evaluation, and many executives are interested in these measures.

Activity or intangibles are defined as positive results that either cannot be converted to monetary values or would involve too much time or expense in the conversion to be worth the effort. The range of intangible outcomes is practically limitless. It is important to note that, even though any of the intangible benefits may not be converted in one evaluation study, they may be converted in another study or in another organization. Not all measures can or should be converted to monetary values. By design, some should be captured and reported as intangible measures. Although they may not be perceived as valuable as the measures converted to monetary values, as stated earlier, intangible or activity-based measures can be important to the overall evaluation process.

In some diversity initiatives such as diversity leadership training, managing multicultural conflict, intangible effects on teamwork, job satisfaction, communication, and customer satisfaction, *etc.*, the intangible or non-monetary benefits can be more important than monetary or tangible measures. Consequently, these measures should be monitored and reported as part of the overall evaluation. In practice, every diversity initiative, regardless of its nature, scope, and content, will have activity-based or intangible measures associated with it. The challenge is to efficiently identify and report them.

A sample of diversity metrics at this level include:

▶ Soft or qualitative measures that cannot be quantified but are important outcomes for the organization.

Figure: 7-2

Typical Intangible Variables Linked with Diversity	
Attitude Survey Data	Employee Transfers
Organizational Commitment	Customer Satisfaction Survey Data
Climate Survey Data	Customer Complaints
Employee Complaints	Customer Response Time
Grievances	Teamwork
Discrimination Complaints	Cooperation
Stress Reduction	Conflict
Employee Turnover	Decisiveness
Employee Absenteeism	Communication
Employee Tardiness	*Etc.*

Compliance Level Diversity Metrics

At bare minimum, organizations must track diversity compliance regarding basic issues of workforce representation, costs of voluntary and involuntary turnover, and financial and other impacts of litigation.

The "Compliance" level diversity metrics are defined as those "demonstrating a weak to moderate commitment to increasing minority representation within the organization." It presupposes cursory attention to diversity in compliance with EEO and Affirmative Action laws or concern with "representation level" mixtures of diverse people in the organization. Compliance level metrics foster a focus on diversity measurement to help assess the impact of the organization's diverse workforce recruiting and retention efforts.

At the compliance level, the commitment to diversity focuses primarily on meeting a representation standard of diversity and avoiding doing things that fail to comply with the law.

A sample of diversity metrics at this level include:

▶ Recruitment, Representation, Voluntary and Involuntary Turnover reduction, and Litigation Exposure Reduction.

Inclusion Level Diversity Metrics

In order to advance your diversity efforts beyond the Compliance level to the third phase, the Inclusion level, it is necessary to focus diversity measurement and analysis at a deeper level that addresses key result areas such as reasonable accommodation, knowledge development, promotion, employee satisfaction, level of senior management commitment, *etc*. This helps move your diversity process from a "maintenance" stage to a "proactive" program.

Compliance level metrics helped lay the basic foundation. Inclusion level metrics help you take an in-depth look at your diversity process change strategy, then advance the process towards building a diversity infrastructure, systems, and capability.

Inclusion level metrics reflect a higher level of commitment to diversity interventions, accompanied by the strong support of senior management and the development of programs designed to build a diversity-friendly environment. It also includes building a diversity focused infrastructure to take advantage of its diverse talent and capability.

In order to build your diversity efforts towards the "Inclusion Level" metrics performance, it is necessary to focus your diversity measurement efforts at an even deeper level that addresses key result areas such as fully represented candidate pools at all levels for promotion and succession planning, diversity-friendly policies, minority and women placements, minority staff who meet competence standards for placement in key assignments, minority and women individual development plans (IDP's) achieved by position and level. It is also important that the definition of diversity and associated metrics are broad and inclusive, capturing all employee segments — gender, race, ethnicity, religion, sexual orientation, disability, *etc*. This helps move the diversity process from a "proactive" stage to an "improved capability" stage that promotes full utilization of all people. It includes a limited use of formal scorecards and diversity focused bonus and incentive plans that support inclusion based metrics.

Inclusion level metrics foster a wider spread utilization of diversity measurement to help assess the impact of diverse workforce promotion, employee satisfaction, building commitment throughout the organization. Inclusion Level metrics help you integrate diversity into the organization's way of operating and utilizing diverse workforce talent and processes as a strategic resource for meeting its goals and objectives.

A sample of diversity metrics at this level include:

▶ Talent Pipeline Development, Retention, Environment and Culture Improvement, Knowledge Development, Work-life Improvement, Succession Planning, Promotion, Employee Satisfaction, Reasonable Accommodation, Leadership Accountability and Commitment, Diversity Initiatives Achievement, Supplier Diversity, and External Recognition, Human Capital Depletion, Compensation Equity, Employee Network Impact, Utilization Rates, *etc.*

Strategic Performance Level Diversity Metrics

In order to advance your diversity efforts beyond the Inclusion level to the fourth phase, the Strategic Performance level, it is necessary to focus diversity measurement and analysis at a level that addresses whether or not your diversity initiatives have had a strategic impact on the organization's business strategy and/or its objectives. In general, examples include reducing or eliminating problems and/or increasing or taking advantage of opportunities.

The *Strategic Performance* level is defined as demonstrating an advanced level of commitment and characterized by the integration and measurement of diversity initiatives for their strategic impact on identified business needs. It also includes the strategic use of scorecards and diversity focused bonus and incentive plans. This helps move the diversity process from an "improved capability" stage to utilizing "strategic capability." It includes the full use of formal scorecards and diversity focused bonus and incentive plans that tie bonus percentage increases and payouts to Strategic Performance metric outcomes and DROI® returns.

A sample of diversity metrics at this level includes:

▶ Productivity Improvement, Innovation, Creativity, Cycle-time Reduction, Market Share Improvement, Customer Retention and Satisfaction, Human Capital Readiness Level, Human Capital Competence Level, Human Capital Commitment Level, Human Capital Satisfaction Level, Climate Impact, and Cost Level, *etc.*

Diversity Return on Investment (DROI®) Level Diversity Metrics

Possibly the ultimate level of evaluation is to compare the financial benefits of a diversity program or initiative to the cost of that initiative. This comparison is the elusive goal of many diversity professionals.

In order to advance your diversity efforts beyond the Strategic Performance level to the fifth phase, the Diversity ROI level, it is necessary to focus diversity measurement and analysis on the financial impact of the diversity initiative.

First, you must have useful techniques to assign values to diversity initiative data, particularly in those areas where it is fairly difficult. Data must be transformed into dollar values before the financial benefit can be calculated. This includes exploring calculations such as the value of increased output (*e.g.*, the average dollar sale, average profit per sale, *etc.*), the value of cost savings (*e.g.*, actual savings in raw materials, supplies, time value of money), the value of time savings (*e.g.*, wages/salaries and benefits saved, reduced training time, penalty avoidance), the value of improved quality (*e.g.*, error reduction, increased accuracy, reduced waste, reduced rework, improved morale, reduced mistakes), and the value of "soft" data (*e.g.*, existing data/historical costs, expert opinion, participant estimation of values/costs, management estimation of values/costs).

Second, the methods of comparisons can be explored, the most common being return on investment (ROI). Using this procedure, Diversity Return on Investment (DROI) can be calculated.

Diversity Return on Investment (DROI)
Level Definition

Return on investment (ROI) may appear to be improper terminology for the diversity field. The expression originates in finance and accounting and usually refers to the pre-tax contribution measured against controllable assets. In formula form it is expressed as:

$$\text{Average ROI} = \frac{\text{pretax earnings}}{\text{average investment}}$$

The *Diversity Return on Investment* level is defined as measuring the anticipated profitability of a diversity initiative investment and its payback period. It is used as a means to measure the performance of an organization's application of diversity in financial terms.

The investment portion of the formula represents capital expenditures such as a training facilities or equipment plus initial development or production costs. The original investment figure can be used or production costs, or the present book value can be expressed as the average investment over a period of time. If the diversity program is a one-time offering, then the figure is the original investment.

However, if the initial costs are spread over a period of time, then the average book value is usually more appropriate. This value is essentially half the initial costs since, through depreciation, a certain fixed part of investment is written off each year over the life of the investment.

For example, in situations where a group of employees are to be trained at one time, the investment figure will be the total cost of analysis, development, delivery, and evaluation lumped together for the bottom part of the equation. The benefits are then calculated assuming that all participants attend the program or have attended the program, depending on whether the return is a prediction or a reflection of what has happened.

To keep calculations simple, it is recommended that the return be based on pretax conditions. This avoids the issue of investment tax credits, depreciation, tax shields, and other related items.

A sample of diversity metrics at this level include:

▶ **DROI® Level (ROI management of metrics)**: DROI®, BCR, and Payback Period

Evaluating the **DROI®** Level provides the greatest challenge to diversity practitioners and professionals. After all, many times our primary objective is to show demonstrated, tangible results from our diversity efforts that is more than the investment costs. However, evaluating **DROI®** and utilizing the Hubbard Diversity Measurement Taxonomy™ (shown in Figure 7-3) is not only possible, it is a routine, structured process of certified diversity professionals trained by the HDM&P Institute.

The Diversity Measurement Performance taxonomy includes the following focus areas:

Figure: 7-3

The Hubbard Five-Level Diversity Measurement Taxonomy™			
by Dr. Edward E. Hubbard, Copyright© 2005, All Rights Reserved			
Rating Level	**Profit Focused Description**	**Government / Non-Profit Description**	**Intangibles –All Levels**
Level I: Organization makes no real attempt to quantify or address diversity measurement as a key performance factor.	· **Activities Focused Level:** Primarily activities, celebrations, slogans, and other programming that is more "event-based" support of diversity. Performance is measured based upon counts such as attendance, number of events held per year, *etc.*	· **Activities Focused Level:** Primarily activities, celebrations, slogans, and other programming that is more "event-based" support of diversity. Performance is measured based upon counts such as attendance, number of events held per year, *etc.*	**All Levels:** Organization consistently demonstrates superior capability in optimizing diverse human capital assets and includes anecdotal as well as quantitative evidence of diversity as a key performance driver
Level II : Organization makes a basic or little attempt to address Diversity Measurement as a key performance factor.	· **Compliance Level (compliance based management of metrics):** Representation, Voluntary and Involuntary Turnover reduction, and Litigation Exposure Reduction.	· **Compliance Level (compliance based management of metrics):** Representation, Voluntary and Involuntary Turnover reduction, and Litigation Exposure Reduction	· **Intangibles Level (anecdotal):** Soft or qualitative measures that cannot be quantified but are important outcomes for the organization.

Figure: 7-3 continued

The Hubbard Five-Level Diversity Measurement Taxonomy™			
by Dr. Edward E. Hubbard, Copyright© 2005, All Rights Reserved			
Rating Level	Profit Focused Description	Government / Non-Profit Description	Intangibles —All Levels
Level III: Organization makes cursory, non-systematic attempts to address at least some components of diversity metrics as a key performance factor. At best, the organization demonstrates adequate, or baseline, capability that form a good foundation for improvement in the organization's performance	**· Inclusion Level (loosely defined use and tracking of metrics):** Talent Pipeline Development, Retention, Environment and Culture Improvement, Knowledge Development, Work-life Improvement, Succession Planning, Promotion, Employee Satisfaction, Reasonable Accommodation, Leadership Accountability and Commitment, Diversity Initiatives Achievement, Supplier Diversity, and External Recognition, Human Capital Depletion, Compensation Equity, Employee Network Impact, Utilization Rates, *etc.*	**· Inclusion Level (loosely defined use and tracking of metrics):** Talent Pipeline Development, Retention, Environment and Culture Improvement, Knowledge Development, Work-life Improvement, Succession Planning, Promotion, Employee Satisfaction, Reasonable Accommodation, Leadership Accountability and Commitment, Diversity Initiatives Achievement, Supplier Diversity, and External Recognition, Human Capital Depletion, Compensation Equity, Employee Network Impact, Utilization Rates, *etc.*	**All Levels:** Organization consistently demonstrates superior capability in optimizing diverse human capital assets and includes anecdotal as well as quantitative evidence of diversity as a key performance driver **· Intangibles Level (anecdotal):** Soft or qualitative measures that cannot be quantified but are important outcomes for the organization.

Figure: 7-3 continued

The Hubbard Five-Level Diversity Measurement Taxonomy™			
by Dr. Edward E. Hubbard, Copyright© 2005, All Rights Reserved			
Rating Level	Profit Focused Description	Government / Non-Profit Description	Intangibles —All Levels
Level IV: Organization is beginning to systematically extend its diversity measurement capability to influence critical performance outcomes and organizational objectives.	· **Strategic Performance Level (strategic performance and scorecard management of metrics):** Productivity Improvement, Innovation, Creativity, Cycle-time Reduction, Market Share Improvement, Customer Retention and Satisfaction, Human Capital Readiness Level, Human Capital Competence Level, Human Capital Commitment Level, Human Capital Satisfaction Level, Climate Impact, and Cost Level, *etc.*	· **Strategic Performance Level (strategic performance and scorecard management of metrics):** Productivity Improvement, Innovation, Creativity, Cycle-time Reduction, Market Share Improvement, Customer Retention and Satisfaction, Human Capital Readiness Level, Human Capital Competence Level, Human Capital Commitment Level, Human Capital Satisfaction Level, Climate Impact, and Cost Level, *etc.*	**All Levels:** Organization consistently demonstrates superior capability in optimizing diverse human capital assets and includes anecdotal as well as quantitative evidence of diversity as a key performance driver · **Intangibles Level (anecdotal):** Soft or qualitative measures that cannot be quantified but are important outcomes for the organization.

Figure: 7-3 continued

The Hubbard Five-Level Diversity Measurement Taxonomy™			
by Dr. Edward E. Hubbard, Copyright© 2005, All Rights Reserved			
Rating Level	Profit Focused Description	Government / Non-Profit Description	Intangibles —All Levels
Level V: Organization consistently demonstrates superior capability in optimizing diverse human capital assets to influence critical performance outcomes and organizational objectives.	· Profit-Focused ROI Level (ROI management of metrics): DROI, BCR	· Mission Focused ROI Level (ROI management of metrics): DROI, BCR	All Levels: Organization consistently demonstrates superior capability in optimizing diverse human capital assets and includes anecdotal as well as quantitative evidence of diversity as a key performance driver · Intangibles Level (anecdotal): Soft or qualitative measures that cannot be quantified but are important outcomes for the organization.

Measurement by the Numbers Is Required

If you want to measure the effects and value of diversity at any level, you can. You can even put a dollar value on the impact. The approaches discussed here are proof that no matter what type of diversity intervention has been applied, it can be measured and evaluated. The most important requirement is that you follow the principles and steps described in this chapter.

If it were easy to measure diversity intervention effects, many more people would be doing this as a matter of routine. When we start to show management exactly how much value diversity efforts can contribute to the process of building an inclusive work environment and performance impact, diversity will become a strategic requirement. As a formal discipline, diversity professionals must approach the work with well-defined standards of care and processes such as those reflected in the Hubbard Diversity Discipline Framework™. They must accept that better performance is the only thing that matters in a competitive organization. And, if you can help better performance happen that results in an improved ROI, you will be seen as adding value to the organization.

CHAPTER 8

Applying the Diversity Discipline's Methodologies

Introduction

The competencies, DAOE's, and roles defined in this book pinpoint the behaviors, knowledge, and responsibilities that are critical for diversity practitioners and professionals. The real value of the Hubbard Diversity Discipline Framework™ competencies, DROI™ processes, and DAOE's is realized in their application. Diversity professionals need to work within their organizations to incorporate the roles, competencies, and DAOE's into efforts to:

▶ attract people into the diversity profession

▶ evaluate individuals for selection or promotion in a diversity job family of positions

▶ diagnose diverse workforce and organization needs

- ▶ design diversity training programs

- ▶ guide diversity career-planning decisions

- ▶ guide coaching and feedback for diversity practitioners

- ▶ assess job performance of diversity practitioners and professionals

- ▶ establish a foundation for diversity credentialing, certification programs, and the like.

The competencies and DAOE's discussed in this book serve as a common framework to build a comprehensive system of diversity related positions and technologies that integrate its application. For example, a hiring manager can use the appropriate competencies and DAOE's to select a new employee who is able to demonstrate the desired competencies and professional expertise to fill a diversity-focused position. Once the individual is hired, the same list of competencies and DAOE's can be used in the performance management system to monitor and evaluate performance on the job. Competencies that are rated as needing improvement can serve as the basis for choosing appropriate training and development activities to build expertise (Bernthal, Paul R; Colteryahn, Karen; Davis, Patty, *et.al.*, 2004). And once diversity professionals know the competencies and DAOE's needed for successful performance, they can become more self-directed in their development.

How to Use the Hubbard Diversity Discipline Framework™ with Clients

The Hubbard Diversity Discipline Framework™ provides business leaders and clients (both external and internal) at all levels with an in-depth profile for success for effective diversity professionals. The model serves as a valuable educational tool for clients. By thoroughly reviewing the competencies, clients can understand how their diversity partners are expected to think strategically and help drive business results. Thus, clients can readily see the potential value of a partnership. For example, clients will understand the Diversity Business Competencies…

▶ Analyzing Needs and Proposing Solutions

▶ Applying Business Understanding

▶ Cost-benefit Analysis

▶ Driving Results

▶ Industry Understanding

▶ Organizational Behavior Understanding

▶ Organizational Development Theories and Techniques Understanding

▶ Organizational Understanding

▶ Thinking Strategically

▶ Planning and Implementing Assignments

- Business Integration Skill

- Change Management Leadership

- Customer Intimacy Skills.

As a result, they can hold their diversity partners accountable for demonstrating these behaviors to help create business focused diversity solutions. Clients are in a unique position to raise the performance bar of the Diversity profession by demanding that its practitioners understand their business, recognize their business priorities, target appropriate improvement opportunities, and make a positive impact on their business results. This understanding will enhance the image of the profession as a legitimate discipline that adds value to the bottom-line.

The Hubbard Diversity Discipline Framework™ also can help clients better understand what's expected of them when identifying and implementing performance-improvement strategies within their own businesses. Being familiar with the roles, DAOE's, and diversity competencies sets expectations for the improvement interaction between clients and the diversity professional. This heightened understanding will increase the client's level of involvement in the implementation and will improve its business impact. Ultimately, true partnering will occur and lead to better bottom-line results. (Bernthal, Paul R; Colteryahn, Karen; Davis, Patty, *et.al.*, 2004)

How Diversity Leaders Can Use the Framework

For Chief Diversity Officers (CDO's) or other Diversity managers, the Hubbard Diversity Discipline Framework™ can serve as a template for success today and in the future. The model may be used to determine which competencies and DAOE's are appropriate for the Diversity Department's operation. Diversity leaders may also use it to assess the extent to which their professionals are demonstrating the competencies and effectively performing in the relevant DAOE's. A comparison of existing talent against the framework will identify individuals' strengths and development needs and those of their particular team.

It is critical that diversity professionals are competent and effective in what they do. This means that leaders ultimately must challenge all diversity professionals to effectively demonstrate all appropriate diversity competencies and any DAOE's within their responsibility. Chances are that such a profile of proficiency is not the current state of affairs and that development, assessment, and coaching will be required of leaders to help their staffs achieve that level of excellence. Diversity leaders are responsible for ensuring that practitioners are competent and held in demand by business leaders. One way to do this is to encourage professionals to expand and enhance their skills.

The Hubbard Diversity Discipline Framework™ is applicable for superior performance both now and in the future. To embrace the future, CDO's and diversity managers need to integrate the competencies and DAOE's into their human performance systems. Doing so raises performance expectations and provides a common link throughout the organization's human resource systems. Integrating the competencies and DAOE's provides a powerful means of ensuring that all systems promote and reinforce the same set of knowledge, skills, and abilities that are important for achieving business results.

CDO's can use the Hubbard Diversity Discipline Framework™ for selection and promotion decisions, training and development needs, career and succession planning inclusion, and performance management. For example, CDO's can include the appropriate competencies or DAOE's in diversity professionals' performance plans, provide feedback on them throughout the year, and rate them in a year-end performance review. For this type of system to be effective, CDO's must make sure the performance management process is balanced; that is, each person's performance plan must include both objectives and competencies/DAOE's. A balanced performance management system ensures employee accountability, clarity, and focus in meeting individual goals, business objectives, and department goals. Diversity professionals need to have a clear understanding of the behaviors that they are expected to display in their daily activities. They also need to know that how they behave (competencies/DAOE's) is just as important as what they achieve (objectives).

How Individual Contributors Can Use

Given the changing composition of the workforce, a
need some level of skill in dealing with diversity. Fo
recently it was announced that White people will no
up the majority of Americans by 2042, according to government
projections. That's eight years sooner than previous estimates
made in 2004. The nation has been growing more diverse for
decades, but the process has sped up through immigration and
higher birth rates among minority residents, especially Hispanics.
According to the Brookings Institute, a think tank in Washington,
D.C., America is also growing older. The White population is older
and very much centered around the aging baby boomers who are
well past their high fertilization years. They state that the future
of America is epitomized by the young people today. They are
basically a melting pot we are going to see in the future. (AOL
News, 2008)

"Am I performing effectively today, and am I ready for the future?"
is the question that every diversity manager and other individual
contributors should be asking. One of the most direct ways to
answer this question is to assess current performance against
the Hubbard Diversity Discipline Framework competency model
competencies. The Hubbard Diversity Discipline Framework
competency model clearly describes what competencies
professionals should have today and in the future.

...ding Your Development Plan: Start with ...elf-Assessment

A good first step is to perform a self-assessment against each set of diversity competencies. This can be done by first reading the competency definition and key actions and then entering the Diversity Professional Competency Profile link shown below: www.hubbardNhubbardinc.com/Diversity_Professional_Profile.htm into your computer browser.

This profile will help you assess yourself by rating your current performance in each Hubbard Diversity Discipline Framework competency model area. For competencies rated as "needs development," you can decide which two or three are most important and then meet with your manager to agree on appropriate developmental activities. The Diversity-focused professional and manager must also discuss the competencies rated as strengths and agree on how best to leverage them for the most profound impact on department and business unit goals.

Diversity professionals and practitioners must position themselves to add quantifiable value to organizational performance. One of the best ways for you to enhance your value to the organization is to take responsibility for your own development. By continually learning and renewing your skills, you will achieve greater versatility, more job satisfaction, and, ultimately, career success and marketability. The Hubbard Diversity Discipline Framework competency model provides an excellent structure for managing current performance, identifying competency gaps, determining developmental needs, measuring progress, and preparing for the future.

Although many diversity practitioners are already viewed as important strategic partners by top executives and line managers, not all are. The profession has the potential to make an even greater difference and to have a more enduring impact in years to come. It is up to each one of us to take action to enhance our skill level to meet the strategic performance needs of our customers. The Hubbard Diversity Discipline Framework competency model will have little value unless it is used to develop professionals further and drive performance higher. The challenge to the profession is clear: Embrace strategic diversity learning and invest in personal development and growth or face extinction as a value-added partner and professional with credibility. By developing your skills, you will help push the diversity profession to higher levels of expertise, credibility, and respect, enabling practitioners to make a measurable difference in helping their customers, clients, and colleagues in the years ahead.

The diversity profession has long championed learning and self-development as an indispensable part of the adult learning experience. The Hubbard Diversity Discipline Framework competency model provides members of the profession with a blueprint for continuous learning. The model also provides a blueprint for success. It enables practitioners to increase their relevance in the business world by sharing accountability for and adding value to their organization's performance. Being viewed as professionals who link diversity efforts to organizational goals and strategies in a meaningful way has never been more critical. It is time for members of the diversity profession to ensure that all strategic diversity change efforts achieve measurable results that align with the organization's strategy. Our success and viability as a profession depends on it!

References

Bernthal, Paul R; Colteryahn, Karen; Davis, Patty; *et.al.*; *Mapping the Future: ASTD 2004 Competency Study*; Virginia, ASTD Press, 2004.

Bauer, I.; Heinl, R.; & McGovern, C.; (2003, June). Consultant Competency Model Role-based Analysis. Pittsburgh, PA. Development Dimensions International

Boyatzis, R., *The Competent Manager: A Model for Effective Performance.* New York: Wiley, 1982.

Brewster, C.; Farndale, E.; & van Ommeren, J.; (2000, June). "HR Competencies and Professional Standards." World Federation of Personnel Management Associations.

Hubbard, Edward E., *How to Calculate Diversity Return on Investment.* California: Global Insights Publishing, 1999.

Hubbard, Edward E., *The Diversity Scorecard.* Massachusetts: Butterworth-Heinemann, Elsevier Publishing, 2004.

Sredl, Henry J.; Rothwell, William J., *Professional Training Roles and Competencies Volume I*, Massachusetts, HRD Press Inc., 1987.

"Whites Fading Fast as Majority in US," AOL News, August 14, 2008.

CHAPTER 9

Maximizing Diversity ROI Performance and Value

Introduction

Management thought-leader Peter Drucker once said that the greatest challenge for organizations for the future will be the shift from an industrial to a knowledge economy. He reminded us that the purpose and function of every organization is the integration of specialized knowledge into a common task. This shift towards knowledge as the differentiator affects all aspects of organization management, including operating efficiency, marketing, organizational structure, and diverse human capital investment. Each of these directly or indirectly hinges on an understanding of the ability of people to cope with individual and other differences, including unforeseen, massive, and usually hurried exchanges with each other. At the end of the day, without hard data on diverse workforce human capital and their impact on work processes, activity, and productivity there is virtually no chance of competing effectively (Fitz-enz, 2000).

Since employee costs can exceed 40 percent of corporate expense, measuring the ROI of diverse human capital is essential. Management and other key stake-holders need a system of diversity measurement and competencies that describe and predict the cost, impact and productivity curves of its workforce. Beyond that and perhaps more important are qualitative measures that capture critical insights concerning workforce initiatives and interventions. Quantitative measures tend to focus on costs, capacity, and time. Qualitative measures focus on value and human reactions. The quantitative measures tell us what happen, whereas the qualitative gives us some idea of why it happened. Together, they offer insights into results and drivers, or causes which help us understand the real value behind the diversity initiative.

Measuring the ROI of diversity has earned a place among the critical issues in the fields of human performance, learning and development, human resources, technology, quality, and marketing. The topic of ROI appears routinely on the agendas of many conferences and professional meetings for other disciplines. Journals and newsletters have been devoting increasing print space to articles about ROI. A professional organization has been developed to exchange information on ROI. At least a dozen books provide detailed coverage of the topic. Even top executives have increased their appetite for ROI information (Phillips and Phillips, 2008).

Measurement of ROI is a much-debated topic. Few business topics stir up emotions to the degree that the ROI issue does. Measuring diversity ROI is characterized as flawed and inappropriate by some, while others describe it as the only answer to their accountability concerns. The truth lies somewhere in the middle. Understanding the drivers of the ROI Methodology and its inherent weaknesses and advantages makes it possible to take a rational approach to the issue and implement an appropriate mix of evaluation strategies that include measuring DROI®.

Although interest in the topic has grown and much progress has been made, ROI is still an issue that challenges even the most sophisticated and progressive organizations. While some professionals argue that calculating ROI is too difficult, others quietly and deliberately develop measures and routinely calculate ROI. The latter group is gaining support from senior management teams. Regardless of the position one takes on the issue, the reasons for measuring ROI are clear. Almost all professionals in the fields mentioned earlier share a concern that they must eventually show a return on investments made in their major programs. If they do not, funds may be reduced or their department or functional unit may not be able to maintain or enhance its present status and influence within the organization.

The measurement dilemma at the heart of the ROI process is a source of frustration for many senior executives. Many executives realize that major processes such as learning, diverse workforce integration, human resources, technology, and marketing are necessary when organizations experience significant growth or increased competition. These processes are also important during business restructuring and rapid change. Executives intuitively feel that these processes add value and logically conclude that they pay off in terms of important bottom-line measures such as productivity improvement, quality enhancement, cost reduction, and time saved, as well as enhanced customer satisfaction, improved morale, and improved teamwork. Yet executives become frustrated with the lack of evidence that shows the actual contributions of initiatives in the fields in which ROI measurement is difficult. The DROI® Methodology represents the most promising way to achieve such accountability through a logical, rational approach; and this methodology is described in this book.

Progress and Status of ROI

The progress and status of ROI varies from field to field. In determining the economic benefit of public projects, cost-benefit analysis has been used for centuries. (Phillips and Phillips, 2008) The same is true for the use of ROI in accounting and finance. In learning and development, ROI evaluations are becoming routine in most organizations. In other fields, such as meetings and events, ROI evaluations are just starting to become frequently used tools for professionals. The diversity field has a way to go to see ROI-based evaluations become routine in most organizations. A recent study conducted by the Hubbard Diversity Measurement & Productivity Institute (DM&P) highlighted that less than 10 percent of respondents are currently using formal processes to calculate the diversity return on investment of their diversity initiatives. Less than 5 percent indicated that they reported on the impact of their diversity interventions using a formal cost-benefit format. This highlights the need for severe improvement in the practice of reporting diversity contributions in an ROI format, the need for the implementation of the Diversity Business Partner and Diversity Performance Consultant/Technologist roles, and routine use of strategic diversity competencies.

At one time, diversity practitioners could use the excuse that a methodology and few tools exist to calculate the return on investment for a perceived "soft" area such as diversity. However, this is simply not the case. Since 1987, Dr. Edward E. Hubbard and the Hubbard Diversity Measurement & Productivity Institute has made available tools, books, software, and a proven diversity return on investment (DROI®) methodology. In fact, the DM&P Institute is dedicated to providing diversity return on investment skills training and consulting worldwide. In addition, diversity is not the "soft" area as perceived previously. A wide array of evidence and case study exist that demonstrates when diversity is utilized strategically, it without a doubt, adds a measurable difference to organizational performance. The Hubbard Diversity Measurement & Productivity Institute has documented and collected a wide range of client and other cases (in the U.S. and abroad) that demonstrate diversity's value-add in financial and non-financial terms.

There are a number of measurement and evaluation schemes that exist with a performance impact focus that are used by diversity practitioners who are serious about tying diversity to organizational performance. The table below, from Phillips, Phillips, Stone, and Burkett (2008) highlight a few examples.

Some of these methods focus on financial success; others on non-financial data; and still others offer a balanced approach to measuring program results.

Measurement and Evaluation Schemes	
Benefit Cost Analysis	Probably the oldest process by which to evaluate feasibility of expenditures of all types of programs is benefit-cost analysis. Based on theoretical frameworks of economics and finance, the original intent of Benefit Cost Analysis (BCA) was to ensure that society maintains the optimal level of efficiency in allocating resources. Since its original use, it has been used to evaluate the success of many types of programs, including training and education.
Kirkpatrick's Four-Level Framework	The most commonly used training and evaluation framework is that developed by Kirkpatrick. Developed in the late 1950's, this framework describes four levels of evaluation: Level 1: reaction; Level 2: learning; Level 3: job behavior; Level 4: results. Many attempts have been made to successfully build on Kirkpatrick's concept of levels.
Phillips' Five-Level ROI Framework	Phillips' ROI methodology and five-level framework is the most widely used process by which to evaluate training and performance improvement programs. Phillips added ROI as the fifth level of evaluation, recognizing that to move from Level 4 to Level 5, Level 4 measures must be converted to monetary value, fully loaded costs must be captured, intangible benefits identified, and the monetary benefits compared to the costs. Hence, this framework combines the Kirkpatrick approach and the Benefit Cost Analysis to ensure a balanced set of measures is reported. Phillips also developed a systematic process that includes a performance-based methodology, strategies, approaches, and tools to implement evaluation at all five levels. The methodology includes the critical step to isolate the effects of the program on key measures from other influences. In addition, the process identifies barriers and enablers to success and provides recommendations for continuous improvement.

Measurement and Evaluation Schemes	
Hubbard Diversity ROI (DROI®) Model Framework and Hubbard Diversity Performance Drivers Model™	Hubbard' DROI® methodology and six-level framework is used to evaluate diversity interventions and performance improvement initiatives. Hubbard added onto the Phillips Framework and created evaluation approaches that are unique to the measurement of diversity and its outcomes. It also recognizes that measures must be converted to monetary value, fully loaded costs must be captured, intangible benefits identified, and the monetary benefits compared to the costs. Hence, this framework combines the Kirkpatrick, Phillips, and Kaplan and Norton Scorecard approaches and the Benefit Cost Analysis to ensure a balanced set of measures is reported. Hubbard also developed a Diversity Performance Drivers Model™ and method which provides a systematic performance-based methodology, strategies, approaches, and tools to implement a strategic return on investment productivity strategy using diverse workforce resources. The methodology includes the critical step to isolate the effects of the diversity initiative on key measures from other influences. In addition, the process identifies barriers and enablers to success and provides recommendations for continuous improvement.
Kaufman's Five Levels of Evaluation	Kaufman expands the Kirkpatrick four-level framework by defining Level 1 as including the concept of enabling, which addresses the availability of various resources and inputs necessary for successful intervention, and by adding a fifth level of evaluation concerned with societal and client responsiveness as well as the consequences and payoffs.
CIRO	Warr, Bird, and Rackham present another four-level framework in which four categories of evaluation make up the CIRO approach. CIRO stands for context, input, reaction, and outcome.

Measurement and Evaluation Schemes	
CIPP	Stufflebeam's CIPP model presents a framework around the program objectives, training content facilitation, program implementation, and program outcomes. CIPP stands for context, input, process, and product.
Marshall and Schriver's Model of Evaluation Knowledge and Skills	This five-step model evaluates knowledge and skills. The five-level model separates the evaluation of knowledge and skills. Level 1 measures participants' attitudes and feelings. Level 2 measures knowledge using paper and pencil tests. Level 3 measures skills and knowledge by requiring participants to demonstrate capability of performing the task's job standards. Level 4 measures skill transfer and Level 5 measures organizational impact and ROI.
Indiana University's Business Impact ISD Model	The evaluation process included in the Business Impact Instructional System's Design Model is based on six strata of impact, beginning with Stratum 0, which accounts for activities such as the volume of training conducted or the number of participants in the program. Stratum 1 measures participants' satisfaction with the program. Stratum 2 measures the extent to which participants exhibit knowledge and skills taught during the program. Stratum 3 measures transfer of the training, answering the question, "Are participants using what they learned?" Stratum 4 measures the extent to which employee performance has improved and whether this improvement affects profitability. Stratum 5 attempts to measure the effect changed performance in organizations has on society.
Success Case Evaluation	Brinkerhoff's success case evaluation uses purposive sampling rather than random sampling to gather data regarding program success. The process focuses on input from training participants who have been most successful as well as least successful in applying the knowledge and skills learned in the program. Through the process, stories of business value evolve as participants describe their success with application and elaborate on the barriers and enablers that either deterred or supported they use of skills and knowledge learned.

Measurement and Evaluation Schemes	
Utility Analysis	The work of Cascio brought utility analysis to the forefront. Utility analysis is a process by which the expected outcomes and the cost of decisions are taken into account. Specific outcomes are defined and the relative importance of the payoff is determined.
Brown and Reed's Integral Framework	This holistic approach to evaluation embraces both individual and organizational learning. Four key concepts to this approach include nested development, referring to the relationship of the participant to the organization; interrelated realms, suggesting that development consider the interaction between the individual and larger groups; the integral framework, suggesting that there are multiple development pathways within each realm; and the link between the development in one realm to the development taking place in another realm.
Balanced Scorecard	A common method used at the organization strategic reporting level, Kaplan and Norton's balanced scorecard presents a framework of an organization's vision from four perspectives (financial, customer, internal business processes, and learning and growth). The intent of the scorecard is to drive strategy for a business unit, such as the training function.

Source: *The ROI Field Book* by Jack J. Phillips, Patti Pullium Phillips, Ron Drew Stone, and Holly Burkett

To maximize diversity's ROI value and performance as well as ensure consistency and replication of diversity impact studies, it is critical that the diversity ROI (DROI®) methodology has operating standards that are applied as the model is used to develop the DROI® studies. The Hubbard DROI® methodology and model fully adopts, integrates, and operates according to the Guiding Principles set forth in the Phillips ROI® Methodology. These Guiding Principles adapted for diversity state the following:

The DROI® Guiding Principles

GUIDING PRINCIPLES
1. When a higher-level evaluation is conducted, data must be collected at lower levels.
2. When an evaluation is planned for a higher level, the previous level of evaluation does not have to be comprehensive.
3. When collecting and analyzing data, use only the most credible source.
4. When analyzing data, choose the most conservative among the alternatives.
5. At least one method must be used to isolate the effects of the solution.
6. If no improvement data are available for a population or from a specific source, it is assumed that little or no improvement has occurred.
7. Estimates of improvements should be adjusted (discounted) for the potential error of the estimate.
8. Extreme data items and unsupported claims should not be used in DROI® calculations.
9. Only the first year of benefits (annual) should be used in the DROI® analysis of short-term solutions.
10. Costs of the solution should be fully loaded for DROI® analysis.
11. Intangible measures are defined as measures that are purposely not converted to monetary values.
12. The results from the DROI® methodology must be communicated to all key stakeholders.

Adapted from source: *The ROI Field Book* by Jack J. Phillips, Patti Pullium Phillips, Ron Drew Stone, and Holly Burkett

These principles help to guide and direct the diversity ROI analysis process as a discipline to build consistency and credibility in the process.

Specific Criteria for an Effective ROI Process

To maximize diversity's ROI performance, value as well as satisfy the needs of critical groups who will evaluate the DROI® process – such as practitioners, senior managers, and researchers – the process of measuring its ROI impact must meet several requirements. Eleven essential criteria for an effective diversity ROI process are described below.

1. The ROI process must be simple—void of complex formulas, lengthy equations, and complicated methodologies. Most ROI evaluation attempts fail to meet this requirement. Some ROI models have become too complex to understand and use because they attempt to obtain statistical perfection and use too many theories. Consequently, they have not been implemented.

2. The ROI process must be *economical* and easy to implement. The process should become a routine part of a diversity initiative's development without requiring significant additional resources. Selecting sample diversity program groups for ROI evaluations and early planning for ROI measurement are often necessary in order to make progress without adding staff.

3. The assumptions, methodology, and techniques must be *credible*. Logical, methodical steps are needed in order to earn the respect of practitioners, senior managers, and researchers. This requires a practical approach to the process.

4. From a researcher's perspective, the ROI process must be *theoretically* sound and based on generally accepted practices. Unfortunately, this requirement can lead to an extensive, complicated process. Ideally, the process will strike a balance between a practical, sensible approach and a sound theoretical basis. This may be one of the toughest challenges for those who wish to develop a model for measuring ROI.

5. The diversity ROI process must *account for factors other than the program* being evaluated that may also have influenced output variables. Isolating the influence of the program or initiative, an issue that is often overlooked, is necessary to build the credibility and accuracy of the process. The ROI process should pinpoint the contribution of the program as opposed to other influences.

6. The diversity ROI process must be appropriate for a *variety of programs*. Some models apply to only a small number of programs, such as multicultural sales or productivity training. Ideally, the process should be applicable to all types of programs.

7. The ROI process must have the *flexibility* to be applied on a pre-program basis as well as a post-program basis. In some situations, an estimate of the ROI is required before the program is developed. Ideally, practitioners should be able to adjust the process for a range of potential time frames.

8. The ROI process must be *applicable to all types of data*— hard data, which typically represent output, quality, costs, and time, as well as soft data, which represent less tangible concepts, such as job satisfaction and customer satisfaction.

9. The ROI process must *include the costs of the program.* The ultimate level of evaluation involves comparing benefits with costs. Although the term ROI has been loosely used to express any benefit of a program or initiative, an acceptable ROI formula must include costs. Omitting or underestimating the costs will destroy the credibility of the ROI values.

10. The actual calculation must use an *acceptable ROI formula.* This formula is often the benefit-cost ratio or the ROI calculation, expressed as a percentage. These formulas compare the actual expenditures for a project with the monetary benefits driven by the project. Although other financial terms may be substituted, using a standard financial calculation in the ROI process is important.

11. Finally, the ROI process must have a *successful track record* in a variety of applications. In far too many situations, models are created but never successfully applied. An effective ROI process should withstand the wear and tear of implementation and get the expected results. (Phillips and Phillips, 2008)

I consider these criteria to be essential; therefore, any diversity ROI methodology should meet most if not all of these criteria. Unfortunately, most diversity ROI processes do not. The good news is that the DROI® Methodology presented in this book meets all of them.

Barriers to ROI Implementation

Although progress has been made in implementation of ROI methodologies, barriers may inhibit its implementation. Some of these barriers are real, and others are myths based on misperceptions. Too often, diversity practitioners use these barriers as reasons for inaction which in turn lessens the credibility of the field. Each barrier is briefly described below.

Financial and Time Costs

The ROI Methodology will add some cost and time to program evaluations, although the added amount will not be excessive. This barrier alone may stop many ROI implementations early in the process. However, a comprehensive ROI process can be implemented for only 3 to 5 percent of a unit's overall budget, and the additional investment in ROI could be offset by the positive results achieved from the programs or the elimination of unproductive or unprofitable programs.

Lack of Staff Skills and Orientation

Many professional diversity staff members do not understand ROI, nor do they have the basic skills necessary to apply the methodology within the scope of their responsibilities. ROI Measurement and evaluation are not usually part of the preparation for staff jobs. Also, programs typically focus on learning outcomes rather than financial results. Diversity staff members often assess results by measuring reaction or learning. Consequently, a major barrier to ROI implementation is the need to orient the diversity staff, change their attitudes, and teach them the necessary skills.

Faulty Needs Assessment

Many programs have been undertaken without an adequate needs assessment. Some of these programs were implemented for the wrong reasons, based on management requests or efforts to chase a popular fad or trend within the industry. If the program is not needed, its benefits will be minimal. An ROI calculation for an unnecessary program will likely yield a negative value. This likelihood deters diversity practitioners from implementing ROI, because they fear facing such a negative reality. More than likely, if the program is not producing the results that key stakeholders and executive are looking for, it will be eliminated eventually with usually a negative reputation to avoid all such programs in the future.

Fear

Some departments and functions do not pursue evaluation of ROI because of fear of failure or fear of the unknown. Fear of failure can manifest in different ways. Diversity designers, developers, facilitators, or program owners may be concerned about the consequence of a negative ROI. They may fear that ROI evaluations will be used as performance evaluation tools to eliminate the diversity department and its personnel instead of as a process improvement tool. Use of the ROI Methodology may be feared due to a dislike of change. This fear of change, often based on unrealistic assumptions and a lack of knowledge, is a real barrier for many ROI implementations.

Lack of Discipline or Planning

Successfully implementing the ROI Methodology requires planning and a disciplined approach in order to keep the process on track. Implementation schedules, evaluation targets, ROI analysis plans, measurement and evaluation policies, and follow-up schedules are required. Diversity staff members may not have enough discipline and determination to stay on course. This lack of staying power can become a barrier, particularly if measuring the diversity ROI is not an immediate requirement. If the current senior management group does not require an ROI evaluation, the diversity staff may not allocate time for the necessary planning and coordination. Only a carefully planned implementation will be successful.

False Assumptions

Many staff members have false assumptions about the ROI process that keep them from attempting diversity ROI implementation. Some typical assumptions are the following:

- ▶ The impact of a program cannot be accurately calculated.

- ▶ Managers do not want to see the results of initiatives and programs expressed in monetary values.

- ▶ If the CEO does not ask for the ROI, he or she does not expect it.

- "I have a professional, competent diversity staff; therefore, I do not have to justify the effectiveness of our programs."

- "Our programs are complex but necessary; therefore, they should not be subjected to an accountability process."

These false assumptions can become real barriers that impede the progress of ROI implementation. (Phillips and Phillips, 2008)

Cautions When Using DROI®

Because of the complexity and sensitivity of the DROI® process, caution is needed when developing, calculating, and communicating the ROI. Implementation of the DROI® process is a very important issue and is a goal of many diversity organizations. Addressing the following issues can help make certain the process does not go off track (Hubbard, 2004).

The DROI® process should be developed for an initiative where a serious needs assessment has been conducted. Because of the evaluation problems that can develop when it is not clear that a need exists, it is recommended that the DROI® study be conducted with initiatives that have had a comprehensive needs assessment; however, some practical considerations and management requests may prohibit this suggested requirement.

The DROI® analysis should always include one or more strategies for isolating the effects of the diversity initiative. Because of the importance of accounting for the influences of other factors, this step in the process must not be ignored. Too often, an excellent study—from what appears to be a very successful diversity effort—is perceived to be worthless because there was no attempt to account for other factors. Omission of this step seriously diminishes the credibility of the diversity initiative study.

When making estimates, use the most reliable and credible sources. Because estimates are critical to any type of analysis, they will usually be an important part of a DROI® study. When they are used, they should be developed properly and obtained from the most reliable and credible sources—those individuals who best understand the overall situation and can provide accurate estimates.

Take a conservative approach when developing both benefits and costs. Conservatism in DROI® analysis builds accuracy and credibility. What matters most is how the target audience perceives the value of the data. A conservative approach is always recommended for both the numerator of the DROI® formula (diversity initiative benefits) and the denominator (diversity initiative costs).

Use caution when comparing the ROI in diversity with other financial returns. There are many ways to calculate the return on funds invested or assets employed. The ROI is just one of them. Although the calculation for DROI® uses the same basic formula as in other investment evaluations, it may not be fully understood by the target group. Its calculation method and its meaning should be clearly communicated. More important, it should be accepted by management as an appropriate measure for measuring diversity results. This kind of credibility must be earned by taking the time to complete all of the assessment and measurement steps in the process.

Involve management in developing the return. Management ultimately makes the decision if a DROI® value is acceptable. To the extent possible, management should be involved in setting parameters for calculations and establishing targets by which diversity initiatives are considered acceptable within the organization.

Approach sensitive and controversial issues with caution. Occasionally, sensitive and controversial issues will be generated when discussing a DROI® value. It is best to avoid debates over what is measurable and what is not measurable unless there is clear evidence of the issue in question. The issue can be included in the overall measurement process as an intangible benefit. Also, some initiatives are so fundamental to the organization's survival that any attempt to measure them is unnecessary. For example, a diversity initiative designed to improve customer service in a customer-focused organization may escape the scrutiny of a DROI® evaluation, on the assumption that if the initiative is well designed, it will improve customer service. As more organizations implement DROI® studies and standards evolve, the diversity measurement discipline will have increasing evidence that DROI® values can be trusted with accuracy and validity.

Develop case studies of your DROI® calculations. Creating case studies of your DROI® interventions can help educate your organization about the full value of your efforts and the benefits in measuring diversity results. These successes and learning opportunities can help other diversity initiatives and other diversity personnel throughout the organization. Hubbard & Hubbard, Inc.'s Diversity Measurement and Productivity Institute offers specific workshops designed to help you develop or turn your existing data into a diversity business case study.

Do not boast about a high return. It is not unusual to generate what appears to be a very high DROI® for a diversity initiative. This can open the diversity organization up to undue criticism and scrutiny even when the numbers are an accurate reflection of the facts. The value for DROI® will be built as more members of the organization come to understand the processes through their own participation on diversity initiative teams and obvious improvements in organizational climate and performance.

Do not try to use DROI® on every diversity initiative. Some diversity initiatives are difficult to quantify, and a DROI® calculation may not be feasible. Other methods of presenting the benefits may be more appropriate. It is helpful to set specific criteria for the selection of diversity initiatives that will be evaluated when using the DROI® level of analyses.

Benefits of Using ROI

This section outlines several important benefits that can be derived from the implementation of the ROI Methodology within an organization.

Measurement of a Diversity Initiative's Contribution

Measuring ROI is the most accurate, credible, and widely used process to show the impact of an initiative. The diversity staff will know the specific contribution from a select number of programs. The ROI will determine whether the benefits of a program, expressed in monetary values, have outweighed the costs. It will determine whether the program made a positive contribution to the organization and whether it was a good investment.

Clear Priorities

Calculating ROI in different areas will determine which programs contribute the most to an organization, allowing priorities to be established for high-impact programs. Successful programs can then be expanded into other areas (if those areas have similar needs) ahead of other programs. Inefficient programs can be redesigned and redeployed. Ineffective programs can be discontinued.

Focus on Results

The DROI® Methodology is a results-based process that requires diversity practitioners, facilitators, participants, and support groups to concentrate on measurable objectives. This process tends to bring a focus on results to all programs, even those not targeted for an ROI evaluation. Thus, DROI® Methodology implementation has the added benefit of improving the effectiveness of all programs.

Respect from Senior Executives and Program Sponsors

Measuring the ROI of diversity initiatives is one of the best ways to earn the respect of your senior management team and your program sponsor. Senior executives always want to see ROI figures. They will appreciate efforts to connect programs with business impact and to show programs' monetary value. The sponsors who support, approve, or initiate programs will view DROI® measurement as a breath of fresh air. They will be able to see an actual value for a program, building confidence in the decision to use the DROI® process.

Positive Changes in Management Perceptions

The DROI® Methodology, when applied consistently and comprehensively, can convince top management that diversity initiatives and programs are investments, not expenses. Managers will see that programs make viable contributions to their objectives, thus increasing their respect for the function or department that produces those programs. Changing perceptions is an important step in building a partnership with management and increasing management support.

ROI Best Practices

Ongoing progress with ROI implementation has provided an opportunity to determine specific strategies that are common among organizations pursuing the ROI Methodology. Several common strategies that are considered the best practices in measurement and evaluation have emerged. Although the following strategies are presented as a comprehensive framework, few organizations have adopted them all. However, parts of the strategy are practiced (Phillips and Phillips, 2008). These practices have been fully adopted and integrated in the application of the Hubbard DROI® Methodology and found to be common in DROI® implementation processes for diversity.

DROI® BEST PRACTICES
1. The DROI® methodology is implemented as a process improvement tool and not a performance evaluation tool for the Diversity staff.
2. DROI® impact studies are conducted very selectively, usually involving 5%-10% of programs.
3. A variety of data collection methods are used in DROI® analysis.
4. For a specific DROI® evaluation, the effects of a Diversity intervention are isolated from other influences.
5. Business impact data are converted to monetary values.
6. DROI® evaluation targets are developed, showing the percentage of programs evaluated at each level.
7. The DROI® methodology generates a micro level scorecard.
8. DROI® methodology data are being integrated to create a macro scorecard for the learning/development function
9. The DROI® methodology is being implemented for about 3%-5% of the Diversity budget.
10. DROI® forecasting is being implemented routinely.
11. The DROI® methodology is used as a tool to strengthen and improve the Diversity /change and intervention process.

Adapted from source: *The ROI Field Book* by Jack J. Phillips, Patti Pullium Phillips, Ron Drew Stone, and Holly Burkett

Final Thoughts

If diversity is to be a formal discipline that is maximized for performance and value, it must operate with a formal framework and roles, specific competencies, rules, guidelines, practices, and cautions. From a measurement standpoint, it must have a formal methodology that is rooted in sound theory and science. This is no different than any other full-fledge discipline. And, like any other disciplines, it must contain a theory and science that is put to the test in real organizational settings to show its forecasted worth and value to contribute to the bottom-line.

Without this kind of litmus test of theory and process applied in "real-life" (that includes specific ROI-based evidence of outcome achievement and value-added), diversity will have difficulty being viewed as a strategic business partner. As professionals, we must learn and use technologies such as the DROI® methodology and the Hubbard Diversity Discipline Framework™ to demonstrate our contribution to the organization's performance and success in both financial and non-financial terms.

With the acceptance of ROI as a mainstream measurement tool for most disciplines, the debate in diversity must shift from *whether or not* the DROI® methodology and the Hubbard Diversity Discipline Framework™ should be implemented. Instead, as a professional discipline it is critical that diversity practitioners perform these analyses on a consistent, standardized basis.

References

Fitz-enz, Jack, *The ROI of Human Capital*. New York, AMACOM, 2000.

Phillips, Jack J.; Phillips, Patti Pullium; Stone, Ron Drew; and Burkett, Holly; *The ROI Field Book*. Massachusetts: Butterworth-Heinemann, Elsevier Publishing, 2007.

Phillips, Patti Pullium, and Phillips, Jack J., *ROI Fundamentals*, New Jersey, John Wiley & Sons, 2008.

Phillips, Jack J.; Stone, Ron D.; and Phillips, Patricia P.; *The Human Resources Scorecard*. Boston: Butterworth–Heinemann, 2001.

Hubbard, Edward E., *The Diversity Scorecard*. Massachusetts: Butterworth-Heinemann, Elsevier Publishing, 2004.

CHAPTER 10

Sustaining and Enhancing the Diversity Profession

Introduction

Performing diversity work as a strategic partner ranks as some of the most important work we can do. It is critical to the myriad of customers served and vital to the people utilized inside the organization that diversity supports. Learning to serve as a strategic partner within the organizational structure is not just a way for diversity practitioners to justify their existence or defend their turf. It has implications for the very survival of the diversity department and of the organization as a whole. If the diversity function cannot show that it adds value, it risks being on the table for reduction, or worse—dismantling. With the right diversity mindset and measurement tools, implementing diversity-strategic business objectives can mean the critical difference between an organization that is just keeping pace with the competition or one major strides ahead. In essence, it requires creating rsity excellence using behavioral and technical apability, demonstrating commitment, and building ...ics of practice to sustain it over time.

In order for an organization to take full advantage of the potential wealth in its diversity mixtures, it must completely embrace the level of diversity required to meet critical organizational challenges head on. This occurs when organizations foster a climate and culture that values differences and maximizes the potential of employees through utilization—in other words, when the organization and the individuals within it operate in a mature fashion.

Achieving Diversity Maturity

According to Dr. R. Roosevelt Thomas (1999), diversity-maturity requires both an individual and organizational set of behaviors that drive success. He states that diversity-mature individuals do the following:

▶ Accept personal responsibility for enhancing their own and their organization's effectiveness.

▶ Demonstrates contextual knowledge (*i.e.*, they know themselves and their organizations and they understand key diversity concepts and definitions).

▶ Are clear about requirements and base include/exclude decisions about differences on how they impact the ability to meet these requirements.

▶ Understand that diversity is accompanied by complexity and tension and are prepared to cope with these in pursuit of greater diversity effectiveness.

▶ Are willing to challenge conventional wisdom.

▶ Engage in continuous learning.

Diversity-mature individuals see themselves, not others, as responsible for addressing diversity effectively. They understand the impact of organizational culture on diversity-related practices, but they do not use it as an excuse for inaction and indifference. Thomas points out that individuals aiming for greater diversity effectiveness would do well to ask themselves the following personal diversity questions:

▶ Am I comfortable working with people from all demographic groups?

▶ Is there a group or groups that I struggle to accept? If so, how have I attempted to overcome my biases?

▶ How will my comfort or lack of comfort with people different from me affect my ability to advance within this workplace?

▶ Do I enjoy diversity? If so, what kind? If so, how much?

Diversity professionals are not exempt from these issues and must answer these questions for themselves. Diversity-mature individuals know that when people with different backgrounds, perspectives, and objectives express themselves openly, there will be tension. This tension is not inherently positive or negative, good or bad; it simply is. Tension that promotes healthy competition can be good. Tension that immobilizes a unit is clearly not. The difficulty is that many individuals, like organizations, are so uncomfortable with tension that they focus on eliminating it rather than managing it. They place more importance on harmony than on achieving objectives.

Diversity-mature individuals learn to function in the face of tension. They know it is not personal but rather part and parcel of the dynamics of diversity. Tension and conflict are not the same. Tension becomes conflict when it is responded to ineptly. Diversity conflict arises when people ask unproductive questions, such as, "What's wrong with you that you aren't more like me?" (Thomas, 1999). Diversity-mature individuals have challenged conventional wisdom and made mindset changes along the way that equip them to respond effectively to these challenges.

By adjusting to this new mindset and accepting personal responsibility for action, diversity practitioners can develop new competencies to fulfill their strategic roles. The new economic paradigm of diversity as a financial contributor requires diversity professionals to do different things and help the organization deal with the dynamic tension that comes with managing a diverse workforce. This means more than just understanding the organization's articulated strategy; it means that diversity professionals must become strategic business partners who comprehend exactly what capabilities, environments, and other factors are needed to drive successful strategy implementation in their organizations and the ways in which diversity affects these components.

To create this center of diversity excellence, diversity-mature individuals must be able to let go of hindering concepts, such as only people with good interpersonal skills can be successful in managing diversity. Good interpersonal skills help, but they are not the sole arbiters of success. Diversity-mature individuals are highly capable of unlearning when needed. Diversity effectiveness requires a willingness and ability to monitor both yourself and the environment, to challenge yourself regularly, and to devise specific ways to work with new concepts so that they eventually become second nature (Thomas, 1999).

Creating Performance Excellence

To create excellence in performance (utilizing diversity), diversity professionals must possess core diversity skills, which are implemented from a strategic framework. These skills, among others, include the following:

Ability to identify diversity mixtures and their related tensions. Because unidentified mixtures cannot be addressed, this is a critical skill. On the surface this skill seems simple and straightforward, yet according to Thomas (1999), many people fail to master it. There is a natural tendency to focus on the diversity mixture that is of most interest to them and to ignore the others. People often overemphasize one diversity dimension such as race or gender at the expense of identifying a critical mixture that may have the most impact on organizational performance.

Ability to analyze mixtures and related tensions. Not all mixtures need to be addressed, only those that interfere with achieving the goal. How key is the mixture? How disruptive are the tensions? Is any action needed? If action is taken, will it significantly enhance meeting the organizational objectives?

Ability to select an appropriate response. If action is needed, what should the action be? In *Redefining Diversity* (1996), Thomas suggests responses from a framework that identifies at least eight choices, including increase/decrease, deny, assimilate, suppress, isolate, tolerate, build future relationships or foster mutual adaptation. Diversity professionals who are skilled in using these responses can quickly sort through the possible options and select the most effective one.

To be effective, diversity professionals must demonstrate a kind of diversity maturity that allows them to internalize key diversity concepts and use them to guide their actions along with integrating the core skills.

Building Diversity ROI Metrics Maturity

Similarly, to be effective at diversity measurement, individuals aiming for greater diversity measurement effectiveness would do well to ask themselves some critical personal questions:

> ▶ Am I comfortable with working with metrics and evaluating data from all demographic groups?

- Are there concepts around measuring diversity, especially beyond race and gender, that I struggle to accept? If so, how have I attempted to overcome my biases?

- How will my comfort or lack of comfort with metrics affect my ability to utilize them within this workplace?

- Do I enjoy diversity measurement? If so, what kind? If so, how much?

- Do I need to hire someone to conduct this portion of our strategic diversity impact analysis or simply support our efforts as a reviewer?

- Do I really want to do the real work required to rigorously apply diversity measures and following the diversity return-on-investment (DROI) process through to its conclusion?

Answers to these questions will help identify any baseline resistance to the diversity measurement process. Sometimes biases toward diversity measurement can come from within our profession and impede setting standards of excellence.

DROI® Community of Practice

To sustain diversity professionals' momentum for excellence and measurement, communities of practice are required. What is a diversity measurement community of practice? It is a group of people who share a concern, set of problems, or a passion for identifying the impact of diversity using measurement processes and who deepen their knowledge and expertise in this area by learning about diversity measurement and interacting on an ongoing basis. They find it useful to compare designs regularly and to discuss the intricacies of their area of interest in diversity measurement. Currently, the Hubbard Diversity Measurement and Productivity Institute (HDM&P) operates a community of practice focused on diversity measurement called the Diversity Return on Investment (DROI®) Forum.

As communities of practice, these people do not necessarily work together every day, but they meet as strategic business partners because they find value in their interactions. As they spend time together, they typically share information, insight, and advice. They help each other solve problems. They discuss their diversity measurement situations, their aspirations, and their needs. They ponder issues, explore ideas, and act as sounding boards. They may create tools, standards, generic designs, manuals, and other documents. However they accumulate knowledge, they become informally bound by the value they find in learning about diversity measurement together. This value is not merely instrumental for their work. It also accrues in personal satisfaction of knowing colleagues who understand each other's perspectives and of belonging to a group of people who enjoy the diversity measurement work. Over time, they develop a unique perspective on the topic as well as a body of common knowledge, practices, and approaches. They may even develop a common sense of identity (Wenger, McDermott, Snyder, 2002). They become a diversity measurement community of practice.

Global Trends in Measurement

A few trends in measurement and evaluation in organizations in both the private and public sectors have been observed on a global basis. The following measurement trends have been identified in our research and are slowly evolving across organizations and cultures in nearly fifty countries. Collectively, these trends have an important impact on the way accountability issues are being addressed.

▶ No longer thought of as an add-on activity, evaluation is an integral part of the design, development, delivery, and implementation of programs.

▶ Organizations are shifting from a reactive approach to a more proactive approach, addressing evaluation early in the cycle.

▶ Measurement and evaluation processes are systematic and methodical, and they are often built into the delivery process, such as by the use of action plans.

▶ Technology is significantly enhancing the measurement and evaluation process, enabling large amounts of data to be collected, processed, analyzed, and integrated across programs.

▶ Evaluation planning is becoming a critical part of the measurement and evaluation cycle because only a carefully planned implementation will be successful.

▶ The implementation of a comprehensive measurement and

evaluation process usually leads to increased emphasis on the initial needs analysis.

▶ Organizations without a comprehensive measurement and evaluation process have often reduced or eliminated their program budgets.

▶ Organizations with comprehensive measurement and evaluation have increased their program budgets.

▶ Use of ROI is emerging as an essential part of the measurement and evaluation process. *ROI* is a familiar term and concept for most executives; therefore they understand ROI and appreciate its usefulness.

▶ Many examples of successful ROI applications are available.

▶ A comprehensive measurement and evaluation process, including measurement of ROI, can be implemented for about 3 or 5 percent of the direct program budget.

As a result, the Diversity field and its practitioners will have much to learn and do to stay credible and current in the eyes of their customers.

Final Thoughts

An effective, measurable business case for diversity must be built on a solid framework of both concept and science through the work of competent, credible diversity professionals using clear standards of excellence linked to business performance. They must view diversity as an integral part of the organizational system. By integrating the ideas underlying diversity with specific measurement strategies and organizational systems theory, diversity professionals can help the organization examine and utilize its diverse resources more dynamically. It is, of course, impossible to predict future events and results; however, we can make better decisions for the future by using tools such as the diversity discipline framework, and the DROI® Methodology to guide us as a basis for discussing how the future might look.

References

Addison Reid, Barbara, "Mentorships Ensure Equal Opportunity." *Personnel Journal*, November 1994, 122–123.

Baytos, Lawrence M., *Designing & Implementing Successful Diversity Programs.* Englewood Cliffs, NJ: Prentice Hall, 1995.

Becker, Brian E.; Huselid, Mark A.; and Ulrich, Dave; *The HR Scorecard: Linking People, Strategy, and Performance.* Boston: Harvard Business School Press, 2001.

Capowski, Genevieve, "Managing Diversity." *Management Review*, 85: 13–19.

Cox, Taylor Jr., *Cultural Diversity in Organizations.* San Francisco: Berrett-Koehler, 1993.

Cox, Taylor, Jr., and Beale, Ruby L., *Developing Competency to Manage Diversity.* San Francisco: Berrett-Koehler, 1997.

Davis, Drew, "Beyond Casual Fridays: Are Managers Tuned in to Workplace Culture?" *Canadian HR Reporter*, May 6, 1996, 17.

Haskett, James L.; Jones, Thomas O.; Loveman, Gary W.; Sasser, Earl W., Jr.; and Schlesinger. Leonard A.; "Putting the Service-Profit Chain to Work." Harvard Business Review, March/April 1994, 164–174.

Haskett, James L.; Sasser, Earl W.; Jr., and Schlesinger, Leonard A.; *The Service Profit Chain.* New York: The Free Press, 1997.

Hubbard, Edward E., *How to Calculate Diversity Return on Investment.* Petaluma, CA: Global Insights, 1999.

Hubbard, Edward E., *Measuring Diversity Results.* Petaluma, CA: Global Insights, 1997.

IBM and Towers Perrin. *Priorities for Competitive Advantage.* New York: IBM and Towers Perrin, 1991.

Kaplan, Robert S., and David P. Norton, *The Balanced Scorecard.* Boston: Harvard Business School Press, 1996.

Lapp, Janet, *Plant Your Feet Firmly in Mid-Air.* Albany, NY: Delmar, 1996.

Loden, Marilyn, *Implementing Diversity.* Chicago: Irwin, 1996.

Loden, Marilyn, and Rosener, Judith, *Workforce America.* Homewood, IL: Business One Irwin, 1991.

Martinez, Michelle Neely, "Equality Effort: Sharpens Bank's Edge." *HR Magazine*, January 1995, 38–43.

Poole, Phebe-Jane, *Diversity: A Business Advantage.* Ajax, Ontario: Poole Publishing, 1997.

Reichheld, Frederick F., and Sasser, Earl W., Jr., "Zero Defections: Quality Comes to Services." *Harvard Business Review*, October 1990.

Rucci, Anthony J.; Kirn, Steven P.; and Quinn, Richard T.; "The Employee-Customer-Profit Chain at Sears." *Harvard Business Review*, 76(1):1998, 90.

Thomas, R. Roosevelt, Jr., *Beyond Race and Gender.* New York: AMACOM, 1991.

Thomas, R. Roosevelt, Jr., *Building a House for Diversity.* New York: AMACOM, 1999.

Thomas, R. Roosevelt, Jr., *Redefining Diversity.* New York: AMACOM, 1996.

See "No More Business as Usual," *Working Woman*, Special Advertising Section: Strength Through Diversity for Bottom-line Success: A Call to Manage Diversity. MacDonald Communications Corporation, March 1999.

Von Eron, Ann M., "Ways to Assess Diversity Success." *HR Magazine*, August 1995, 51–60.

Wenger, Etienne; McDermott, Richard; and Snyder, William M.; *Cultivating Communities of Practice.* Boston: Harvard Business School Press, 2002.

Index

A

Activities Focused Level, 150, 151, 164

Activity-Level, 155

ADA, 113

affinity group, 57

affirmative action, 30, 31, 81

Affirmative Action, 150, 152, 157

Alignment, 100

AOEs, 88, 89, 92, 93, 99

Areas of Expertise, 17, 49, 50, 51, 52, 72, 88, 90, 100

Awareness and Start-up, 59

B

Balanced Scorecard, 191, 223

BCR, 142, 163, 168

Behavioral Diversity, 26, 131

Benefits, 141, 142, 144

Brookings Institute, 177

Building Strategic Capability, 59

Business and Global Diversity, 26, 27, 131, 132

Business Competencies, 53, 75, 115, 173

C

certification, 13, 14, 15, 20, 33, 35, 36, 37, 38, 172

Certified Diversity Advisor® (CDA), 15, 38

Certified Diversity Business Partner® (CDBP), 15, 38

Certified Diversity Intervention Specialist® (CDIS), 15, 38

Certified Diversity Performance Consultant® (CDPC), 15, 38

Certified Diversity Strategist® (CDS), 15, 38

Certified Diversity Trainer® (CDT), 15, 38

Chief Diversity Officer, 50, 56, 67, 70, 105

CIPP, 189

Collect Data And Analyze It, 136

competency model, 17, 22, 23, 24, 45, 48, 88, 105, 108, 177, 178, 179

Compliance, 150, 152, 154, 157, 158, 164

Control groups, 138

Convert The Contribution To Money, 139

cost of quality, 139

cost/benefit analysis, 141

CPT, 14, 37

Creating a Measurable Diversity Strategic Plan, 35

Customer inputs, 138

D

DAOE, 49, 50

DAOEs, 17, 88, 100, 171, 172, 174, 175, 176

Diversity, 26

Diversity Advisor, 15, 38, 69

The Author

Dr. Edward E. Hubbard is President and CEO of Hubbard & Hubbard, Inc., Petaluma, CA, an international organization and human performance-consulting corporation that specializes in techniques for applied business performance improvement, workforce diversity measurement, instructional design and organizational development.

He is the founder of the Hubbard Diversity Measurement and Productivity Institute and is also author of more than 40 books including the groundbreaking books: *Measuring Diversity Results*, *How to Calculate Diversity Return-on-Investment*, *Pathways to Diversity Metrics for Corporate Legal and Law Firms*, *The Diversity Scorecard*, *Implementing Diversity Measurement and Management*, and the *Manager's Pocket Guide to Diversity Management*.

Dr. Hubbard is one of the first metrics authors in the field of diversity. As a result of his extensive research in the area of diversity measurement and expertise in computer programming, he is one of the first to develop automated software technologies for measuring diversity return-on-investment and performance improvements.

He has performed client work in organizational change and diverse workforce integration for private Fortune 500 companies, the U.S. Government, and corporate clients in the Far East, the Netherlands, other parts of Europe, Hawaii, Samoa, and locations throughout the Pacific Rim and the Federated States of Micronesia. His work includes assisting organizations with issues such as diverse workforce integration, staff development, quality improvement, performance improvement strategies, and restructuring work teams to utilize the strengths of a multi-ethnic workforce. Additionally, work in these countries include strategic planning and analysis, workforce recruitment and retention strategies, diversity return-on-investment metrics and methods, succession planning and development, as well as full scale organization development interventions.

Dr. Hubbard is an internationally known and respected business consultant, trainer, former professor and Director at Ohio State University, a business professional at several Fortune 100 corporations, such as Computer Systems Analyst, Xerox Corporation and the Informatics Corporation, Computer Room Operations Manager, Battelle Memorial Institute, Internal Consultant and Education Specialist, Mead Corporation, and Corporate Director, Training, Organization Development and Compensation for the 17 billion dollar McKesson Corporation.

The July/August 2007 Issue of *Profiles in Diversity Journal* featured Dr. Hubbard as the "Diversity Pioneer" in Diversity Measurement. The American Society for Training and Development (ASTD) inducted Dr. Ed Hubbard into the prestigious "ASTD New Guard for 2003." The New Guard represents selected "members of the Training and Development profession who are taking themselves and the field in new directions." He serves as a Editorial Advisory Board member of Strategic Diversity & Inclusion Management (SDIM magazine and has served as a member of the ASTD ROI Advisory Board. In addition, Dr. Hubbard received double honors being named to the prestigious *Who's Who in Leading*

American Executives and *Who's Who Worldwide of Global Business Leaders*. Memberships are limited to those individuals who have demonstrated outstanding leadership and achievement in their occupation, industry or profession. Some of Dr. Hubbard's other book titles include: *The Hidden Side of Employee Resistance To Change, Managing Customer Service on the Frontline, Managing Your Business For Profitable Growth, Hiring Strategies For Long-Term Success, How To Start Your Own Business With Empty Pockets, Managing Organizational Change: Strategies For Building Commitment.*

Articles by Dr. Hubbard have appeared in magazines and newspapers such as *Inc. Magazine, Fortune, Forbes, Cultural Diversity at Work, Next Step Magazine, American Society for Training and Development Journal, Society for Human Resources Management (SHRM) HR Magazine, Sonoma Business Magazine, Organization Development Network Journal, The Cleveland Plain Dealer, Strategic Diversity & Inclusion Management (SDIM)* magazine (where he serves as a Board Member), *The Diversity Factor Magazine, Diversity Inc.,* and many others. He has also been featured in several business films and management development videos, on radio programs, and is a regularly featured speaker, and keynote for national and international conferences, tele-conferences, seminars, and workshops.

A brief list of Hubbard & Hubbard, Inc. clients include Prudential Financial, Starbucks, Inc., McDonalds Corporation, M.D. Anderson Cancer Center, Kaiser Permanente, America Online, key military leaders at the Pentagon, U.S. and abroad, and many others.

Dr. Hubbard is an expert in Organizational Behavior, Organizational Analysis, Applied Performance Improvement and Measurement Strategies, Strategic Planning, Diversity Measurement, and Organizational Change Methodologies. He holds a Practitioner Certification and Master Practitioner Certification in Neurolinguistic Programming (NLP). Dr. Hubbard earned Bachelors and Masters Degrees from Ohio State University and earned a Ph.D. with Honors in Business Administration.

Books by Dr. Edward E. Hubbard

MEASURING DIVERSITY RESULTS

gives you a reliable, work-tested system of data collection and diversity and productivity measurement tools that will feed back the organization's progress through solid, factual results. In this ground-breaking book, Dr. Hubbard takes you through the mechanics of creating simple mathematical formulas and advanced calculations and approaches for measuring the efficiency and effectiveness of key Diversity change efforts.

Cost: $ 34.95   Order# HH-1-883733-17-0   Book & Software COMBO: $ 149.00

HOW TO CALCULATE DIVERSITY RETURN ON INVESTMENT

is a timely and cutting edge book that enhances on Dr. Hubbard's earlier book Measuring Diversity Results. In this book, he helps you demonstrate diversity's link to dollar ROI in a step-by-step format that is easy to apply. You are provided with a concrete road map with detailed instructions to design, measure, analyze, and/or improve diversity initiatives' impact and demonstrate its financial return on investment.

Cost: $ 42.95   Order# HH-1-883733-21-9

THE DIVERSITY SCORECARD: Evaluating the Impact of Diversity on Organizational Performance

This book by Dr. Edward Hubbard demonstrates his continued commitment to the field of diversity and ROI. It is designed to provide step-by-step instructions, worksheets and examples to help diversity executives and managers analyze and track the impact of their diversity initiatives to mobilize the organization for strategic culture change. Diversity professionals know they must begin to show how diversity is linked to the bottom-line in hard numbers or they will have difficulty maintaining funds, gaining support, and obtaining resources to generate progress.

The Diversity Scorecard focuses on tools and techniques to make sure diversity professionals collect the right type of data that will help ensure the organization's success both now and in the future. To further your learning, Dr. Hubbard has created the Diversity Measurement & Productivity Institute (DM&P) which offers regularly scheduled workshops that are built around the skills and techniques provided in his various research-based books.

Cost: $39.99   Order# BH-0-7506-7457-1   Book & Software COMBO: $410.00

IMPLEMENTING DIVERSITY MEASUREMENT AND MANAGEMENT

Casebook Volume 1 of the Diversity in Practice series edited by Dr. Edward Hubbard shows case after case of diversity professionals highlighting how their work in diversity is making a significant difference and financial impact on organization's performance. This 400-page book is divided into two parts. Part one concentrates on diversity measurement applications which demonstrates diversity's financial impact. Part two highlights the practical approaches in diversity management that build strategic capability for the organization. If you are interested in being recognized for your work in diversity by writing a case, contact Hubbard & Hubbard, Inc. we welcome your contribution to the field of diversity

Cost: $ 44.95   Order# HH-1-883733-24-3

THE MANAGER'S POCKET GUIDE TO DIVERSITY MANAGEMENT

is designed to help you build diversity management skills to create a high performing work environment. It is meant be used as an interactive workbook to test your skills, teach or reinforce diversity concepts, and provide techniques to utilize a diverse workforce to improve organizational performance.

Cost: $ 12.95   Item# HRD-MPGDM

DIVERSITY PERFORMANCE CONSULTING

Providing diversity professionals with a strategic step-by-step diversity consulting process. Publication scheduled for March 2009.. Diversity Performance Consulting will help you take a disciplined performance analysis approach to assessing individual and organizational effectiveness. It will teach you how to apply tools and techniques to diagnose causes of diversity tensions from differences, similarities and complexities, utilize diversity strategies to drive organizational performance, and provide recommendations to implement a set of interventions. The approach is based on a body of knowledge about diversity, diversity management and utilizes applied sciences of organization and human performance technologies. It is jammed-packed with tools, templates, step-by-step methods that offer advice on how to improve the utilization of appropriate diversity mixtures for effective organizational and people performance.

Diversity Performance Consulting is a specialized discipline within the field of diversity consulting. This book will help you learn how to operate as a true diversity performance consultant. It will offer advice and tools to help you...

• Operate as an expert in diversity analysis, diversity measurement and diversity return on investment (DROI®) technologies and provide expert advice.

- Play multiple strategic roles to meet organizational performance needs.
- Be seen as a credible and valuable strategic business partner
- Avoid being predisposed towards a particular solution and wait to make recommendations when data is available to support the most effective solution
- Focus on outcomes and measured quantitative and qualitative results that affect mission and business performance
- Guide the implementation of solutions to organizational performance problems
- And much more!

Cost: $ 44.95   Order# HH-1-883733-28-6

MEASURING THE ROI IMPACT OF DIVERSITY TRAINING

Any Diversity Professional who desires to meet the full requirements of a true strategic business partner must have the skill to show a measurable return on the organization's training investment. After you have trained hundreds or thousands of employees on diversity and inclusion practices, "C-Suite" executives and others will want to know "What is the value and impact that we have received for the dollars invested"? How well would you be able to explain and show this in measured outcomes and results?

This timely, cutting edge book applies proven training evaluation and Diversity ROI evaluation processes created by recognized diversity measurement pioneer Dr. Edward E. Hubbard. It will help you assess the impact and success of your diversity training initiatives. Dr. Hubbard will help you demonstrate diversity's link to dollar ROI in a step-by-step format that is easy to apply. You are provided with a concrete road map with detailed instructions to design, measure, analyze, and/or improve diversity initiatives' impact and demonstrate your Training Return on Investment (TROI™). *Publication scheduled for June 2009..*

Cost: $ 42.95   Order# HH-1-883733-30-8

A Sampling of Tools and Services from Hubbard and Hubbard, Inc.

DIVERSITY PROFESSIONAL CERTIFICATION

The Hubbard Diversity Measurement and Productivity (HDM&P) Institute offers six diversity certifications based in its Diversity ROI® and Diversity ROI Analytics® methodology:

▶ Certified Diversity Trainer® (CDT)

▶ Certified Diversity Advisor® (CDA)

▶ Certified Diversity Performance Consultant® (CDPC)

▶ Certified Diversity Business Partner® (CDBP)

▶ Certified Diversity Strategist® (CDS)

▶ Certified Diversity Intervention Specialist® (CDIS)

Please go to our website **www.hubbardNhubbardinc.com** for additional information about the certification process and a schedule of certification workshops and programs.

Hubbard & Hubbard, Inc. established the Hubbard Measurement & Productivity Institute (DM&P) to provide measurement skills, certification workshops and applied learning conferences for assessing, measuring and evaluating diversity results and diversity return on investment DROI® impact in organizations.

Based on the ground-breaking research by Dr. Edward E. Hubbard, this institute is dedicated to assisting practitioners and other professionals with tools and techniques to research, develop, apply and evaluate measurable organizational solutions for strategic performance improvement. The Institute conducts a wide range of diversity return on investment studies and develops diversity business case examples which clearly demonstrate their impact on bottom-line business or organizational objectives.

Our mission is to provide leading-edge tools diversity professionals need to make effective, timely decisions to create a measurable performance impact!

HUBBARD
Diversity ROI
INSTITUTE

Although interest in measuring the return on investment (DROI)
effects of diversity has been growing, the topic still challenges
even the most sophisticated and progressive diversity organizations
and professionals.

These professionals know they must begin to show how diversity
is linked to bottom-line ROI performance or they will have
difficulty maintaining funding, gaining support, and assessing
progress. The Hubbard Diversity ROI Institute™ (HDROI™)
provides on-going, solution-based skill building in the use of
DROI Analytics® with a focus on measuring organizational
productivity, performance and results. We offer diversity analytics
training, consulting, measurement skills, certification workshops
and applied learning conferences. Our mission is to provide the
most up-to-date analytics tools, techniques and processes diversity
professionals need to make effective, timely decisions to create a
measurable performance impact!

Hubbard & Hubbard, Inc., has created and distributes several Easy-to-Use automated measurement products and software systems that put the power of measurement technology at your fingertips!

MetricLINK® A Comprehensive Performance Measurement & Management System for Organizational Excellence

The MetricLINK® measurement system is extremely flexible and can be used in a wide variety of applications. It can be used to Design, Measure, Manage, Report, and Track Measures in a wide variety of industries and can be applied in uses such as...

Private Industry	Government	Non-Profit	Community
Balanced Scorecard Statistics	Balanced Scorecard Statistics	Healthcare Statistics	Volunteerism Scorecard Statistics
Quality Scorecard Statistics	Quality Scorecard Statistics	Patient Care Statistics	Community Impact Statistics
Team Performance Statistics	Team Performance Statistics	Team Performance Statistics	Donation & Philanthropy Statistics
Diversity Scorecard	Diversity Scorecard	Diversity Scorecard	Diversity Scorecard
Six Sigma Metrics	Six Sigma Metrics	Six Sigma Metrics	Safety Statistics
Human Resources Scorecard	Human Resources Scorecard	Human Resources Scorecard	Six Sigma Metrics
Process Management Scorecard	Process Management Scorecard	Productivity Improvement Statistics	Productivity Improvement Statistics
Organizational Effectiveness & Efficiency Statistics	Organizational Effectiveness Efficiency Statistics	Donation & Philanthropy Statistics	Organizational Effectiveness & Efficiency Statistics
Productivity Improvement Statistics	Safety Statistics	Student Performance Metrics	Safety Statistics
Manufacturing Statistics	Customer Satisfaction Statistics	Customer Satisfaction Statistics	Process Management Scorecard

Hubbard & Hubbard, Inc., offers standardized and custom diversity measurement services, including:

- Diversity Scorecards
  building strategic measurement tools for reporting the impact of your diversity initiatives

- Diversity Initiative
  Impact/ROI Analysis
  calculating the financial impact of your diversity initiatives

- Diversity Dashboards
  creating interactive, graphic displays of your diversity ROI result

- Diversity Culture and
  Systems Audits
  assessing the diversity climate and culture

- Diverse Work Team
  Impact Analysis
  analyzing the effectiveness of your diverse work teams

- Global Diversity Metrics
  providing a numerical breakdown of your world-wide diversity initiatives' impact

- Diversity Council Impact Analysis
  assessing the effectiveness of your diversity council

- Diversity Strategic
  Planning Development
  creating a strategic plan for implementing your company's diversity goals

- DROI™ Analytics™
  creating a strategic diversity measurement framework for assessing and benchmarking your diversity progress

DIVERSITY INSIGHTS PROFILE

The workplace is changing to reflect a highly diverse workforce. To be effective, organizations and their employees must be able to understand, accept, and capitalize on differences. The Diversity Insights Profile® provides a safe, confidential way for employees to explore complex diversity issues and their perceptions across two key dimensions: Diversity Comprehension and Behavioral Performance.

This research-based assessment instrument is a self-scoring tool which helps employees examine their perceptions and "cultural programming" to provide "insight" into their current level of knowledge and skill when interacting with people who are different than themselves. It is designed for organizations and individuals interested in developing and/or improving interpersonal interactions.

It contains interpretation and analysis to help employees calculate and summarize the impact of their responses as well provides detailed Action Planning worksheets for improvement. The feedback resulting from this instrument will increase awareness of individual, ethnic, and cultural differences and identify potential areas for improvement. Spanish Version also available.

Cost: 5-Pak $69.95 Order# HH-DIP-5PK

SKILL-BUILDING WORKSHOPS

Please go to **www.hubbardNhubbardinc.com** for descriptions and scheduling of workshops and webinars.

LIVE PRESENTATIONS

Dr. Hubbard is available for conference presentations, internal workshops, and consulting.

Please call Myra Hubbard: 707-481-2268 or email: myrahub@aol.com to schedule in-person time with Dr. Hubbard for your company.